Creative Tape Recording

For
Jane and Andrew

Master
Creative Tape Recording

John Gardner

Newnes Technical Books

Hayden Book Company, Inc.

The Butterworth Group

United Kingdom

Butterworth & Co (Publishers) Ltd
London: 88 Kingsway, WC2B 6AB

Australia

Butterworths Pty Ltd
Sydney: 586 Pacific Highway, NSW 2067
Also at Melbourne, Brisbane, Adelaide and Perth

New Zealand

Butterworths of New Zealand Ltd
Wellington: 26-28 Waring Taylor Street, 1

South Africa

Butterworth & Co (South Africa) (Pty) Ltd
Durban: 152-154 Gale Street

USA and Canada

Hayden Book Company, Inc
50 Essex Street
Rochelle Park
New Jersey 07662

Library of Congress Catalog Card Number 77-74636

First published in 1977 by
Newnes Technical Books, a Butterworth imprint,
and
Hayden Book Company, Inc

Copyright © by Butterworth & Co (Publishers) Ltd, 1977

UK and all countries outside North America: ISBN 0 408 00244 1
USA and Canada: ISBN 0 8104 0843-0

Typeset by Cold Composition Ltd, Tonbridge, Kent
Printed in England by Butler & Tanner Ltd, Frome and London

Preface

It is probably true to say that out of every hundred people who take up recording as a hobby, only four or five ever achieve any real satisfaction as a result of their efforts and continue with the hobby for any length of time. There is a familiar progression from initial enthusiasm and quite heavy capital outlay through disappointment and disillusion to the disposal of the equipment, or its relegation to the role of an occasional toy.

One does not have to be outstandingly clever to operate a tape recorder, to use a mixer or to choose the right microphone for a particular application. What is required is a degree of manual dexterity and a basic understanding of what the equipment will do. There is no shortage of people who can operate the equipment, nor, it seems, is there a shortage of creative talent, particularly amongst young people. Unfortunately the happy fusion of technical and creative talent is more rare and early failures, for whatever reason, frequently blunt the edge of early enthusiasm.

The tape recorder is a remarkable creative tool and a considerable technical achievement, and having been professionally associated with it on both levels for many years, it seems sad to me that so many people should be unable to realise the potential of the tape medium. The reason for failure is not necessarily lack of skill nor of knowledge but the inability to apply one's talent to the project in hand. Creative recording is based on relatively few basic principles, and much of one's knowledge tends to be gained from fellow enthusiasts, some of whom may be suspect in their own grasp of the subject!

Master Creative Tape Recording presents the basic foundations of the subject without labouring technical details any more than is essential for an understanding of a particular topic. It can either be read in sequence or dipped into as required: the first chapter on the principles of tape recording is included for the sake of completeness, but it is the only chapter which deals with theory rather than practice and the author will not be mortally offended if the reader begins with Chapter 2.

The contents follow a more or less logical progression, from the hardware to its application and operation in a variety of typical situations. Much of the content has been suggested by queries from readers of my articles in various technical magazines, to whom I am indebted for their interest and encouragement.

Contents

1. Recording and reproduction

A magnetic tape is to a recording system what a sheet of paper is to a pen: it is a medium for the storage of information. If a pen writes words in a given order, say from left to right, then the eye recovers the original message by sequentially scanning the paper in a similar manner. In the case of a tape recorder a stationary head 'writes' a magnetic message on a moving tape which traverses it at constant speed. The stored message is an invisible one composed effectively of a series of magnets varying in length and strength. To 'read' the message, the tape is wound back and replayed at the original speed and scanned by a reproducing head.

The Tape

The tape has a thin, pliable base such as Mylar, polyester, p.v.c. or other similarly derived plastics material: polyester is most commonly used and the base thickness of standard tape is about two thousandths of an inch, or 50 μm (1 μm = 1 millionth of a metre). The base is coated with a magnetic oxide powder of minute needle-shaped particles, and there are two oxides which have particularly good properties for magnetic recording. The first is gamma ferric oxide (Fe_2O_3), which is not a naturally occurring substance and has to be derived from the non-magnetic alpha ferric oxide. The second is chromium dioxide (CrO_2) and is a comparatively recent development in magnetic recording. It first appeared in 1966 but did not become a commercial proposition until the rapid expansion of the cassette market.

CrO_2 tape has very different characteristics from 'standard' tape and few of the early cassette recorders were designed to take advantage of its properties. It has a finer and more regular particle structure than ferric oxide tape, giving improved high frequency performance, especially at low speeds.

Each type of oxide must be applied to its base material under critically controlled conditions to form an even coating about 0.16 thousandths of an inch (4 μm) thick. To give the necessary adhesion, the oxide is mixed with a binder, a solvent and a lubricant, forming a magnetic paste or *dope*. At this stage of manufacture the particles are given a common orientation so that the tape has a type of grain, which for conventional sound recording is horizontal. Aligning the particles in this manner allows a more concentrated coating to be applied than if they were

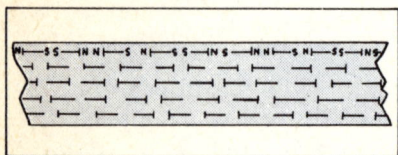

Magnetic tape has a 'grain', but in the demagnetised state the distribution of polarity is random.

scattered in a random fashion. For a given type of oxide and a given tape width, the thickness of the tape coating determines the maximum output possible from the tape. We will return later to the method by which the tape is recorded and replayed.

The Recording System

In order to convert the incoming audio signals into a form which can be accurately transferred to the tape, a machine is required to provide the necessary electrical processing circuits and also to transport the tape at constant speed.

What happens is that an audio signal, in the form of a varying voltage, such as might be obtained from a record player or a microphone, is fed to the input of the tape recorder. This signal is amplified and fed via a record level control to a further amplifier which has an unusual frequency characteristic and is called an *equaliser*. Usually one expects high fidelity equipment to have a flat frequency response and treat all signals equally. The response of the recording amplifier is not flat because certain losses occur in converting electrical energy to magnetic and vice versa, and the amplifier is tailored to compensate for some of these losses. It will

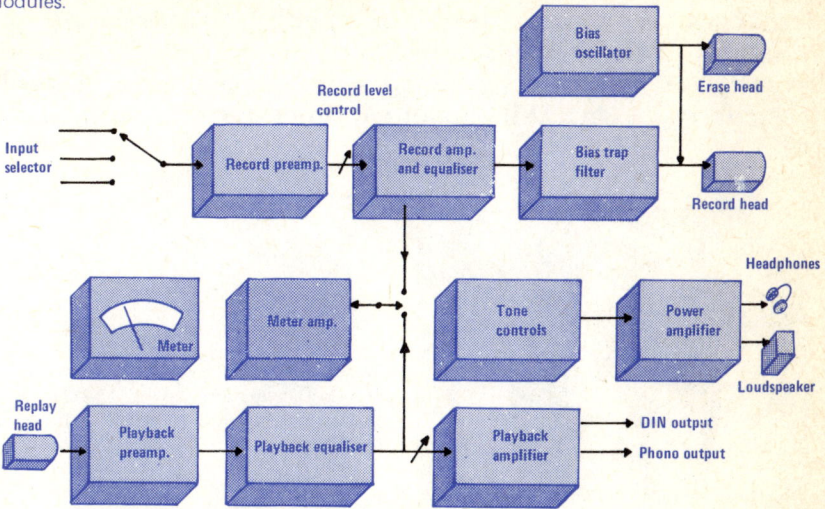

Simplified block diagram of a three-headed tape recorder, showing the main electronic modules.

be seen from the response of a typical recording amplifier that the high frequencies are boosted considerably. Because of this, care has to be taken to ensure that the tape is not overloaded (or saturated) by high energy, high frequency signals. For this reason it is usual to have a level meter or other form of indicator to show the relative level being fed to the recording head. Some machines have meters which precede the equaliser stage, and although these will indicate the nature of the incoming audio signal they will not so accurately give a warning of possible tape overload.

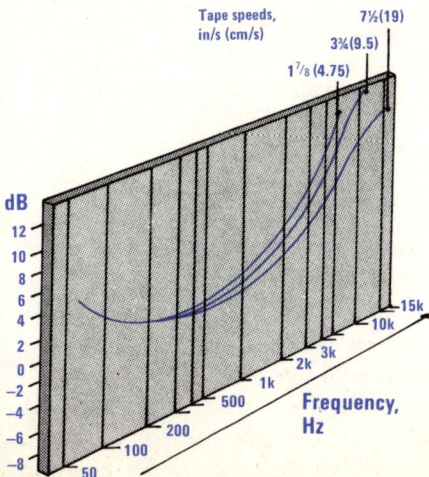

Response curves of a typical recording amplifier. Considerable high frequency boost is applied, more boost being required at low than at high speeds.

3

To store the amplified and equalised audio signal on tape it must be converted into a form which the tape will recognise and retain. This conversion is carried out by the tape head. In essence this is a ring-shaped electromagnet: it has a core with a pair of machined pole pieces, separated by a small non-magnetic shim. Usually there is also a back shim about ten times the width of the front one.

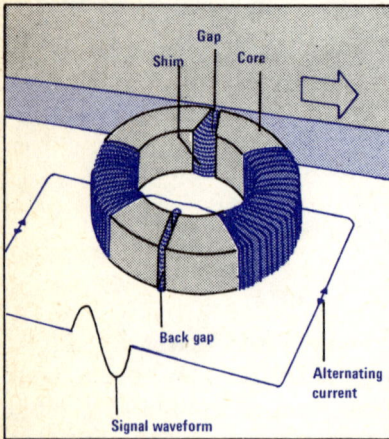

Theoretical construction of a tape head. Varying signal currents in the head winding produce a varying magnetic flux across the front gap.

After passing through the various stages of amplification and equalisation shown on page 3, the audio signal, in the form of a varying voltage, is applied to the winding of the tape head. Now, if a current flows through a piece of wire, a magnetic field is created around the wire and if the wire is wound into a coil this field is intensified. If we now insert a core such as soft iron into the coil, the iron will become magnetised and remain so until the voltage applied to the coil is removed. A tape head is simply a variation of this idea with the coil curved to bring the two ends (or poles) into close proximity.

With a constant voltage applied to the coil, the iron core will have a north and a south pole, rather like a horseshoe magnet. If the polarity of the supply voltage is reversed, by changing over the positive and negative connections to the battery, the two poles will be reversed: north will become south and vice versa. This will only happen, as we shall see shortly, if the core is made from a particular type of material which remains magnetised only for as long as the voltage is applied to the coil. Always remember that in practice a d.c. supply such as a battery should never be applied to the winding of a tape head, as there is a

4

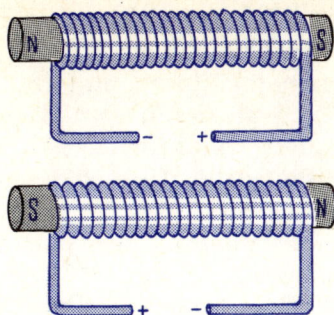

If a soft iron core is inserted into a coil of wire through which a current is flowing, the core will be magnetised. One end will have south polarity and the other north polarity. If the direction of current flow is reversed, the polarity of the core will reverse.

danger that the core will be permanently magnetised and ruin subsequent recordings. For this reason an ohmmeter should never be used to test the continuity of a tape head.

If we substitute for the battery the varying audio signal from the recording amplifier, then the poles will alternate in sympathy with the positive and negative half-cycles of the applied signal. The strength of the poles at any instant will depend on the amplitude of the signal, which in turn depends on the loudness of the original sound. Because of the shim at the front of the head, which fills the gap between the pole pieces, the magnetic flux cannot easily pass from the north to the south pole. In fact the reluctance of the shim (reluctance is the magnetic equivalent of resistance) is so high that it is easier for the flux to complete the magnetic circuit by crossing the air space between the poles.

We can see, then, that if the recording tape is drawn across the face of the head whilst a signal is applied, it will be subjected to the influence of the varying flux pattern in front of the shim.

Now we must explain an apparent anomaly: the tape head remains magnetised only for as long as a voltage is applied to the windings, yet the tape oxide remains magnetised until it is deliberately demagnetised. The explanation for this lies in the

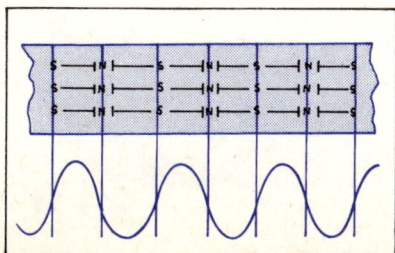

A constant tone input signal would effectively produce a series of bar magnets of equal length along the tape.

fact that there are two types of magnetic material: one is magnetically *soft* and the other is magnetically *hard*. A soft material will react quickly to changes in magnetic force and when that force is removed it will retain very little magnetism. This ability to react rapidly to changing magnetic conditions is exactly what is required of a tape head and, consequently, it is made from soft material such as mumetal, permalloy, soft iron or one of the more recent ferro-ceramic materials. A hard material will retain a large proportion of induced magnetism and that which is retained cannot easily be erased. Recording tape, therefore, is magnetically hard.

Earlier we established that the tape is made of a plastics base coated with an oxide powder. Low noise, high output tapes have a finer granular structure and a denser particle distribution than standard tapes. When the tape is in a so-called demagnetised state the individual particles, which resemble minute bar magnets,

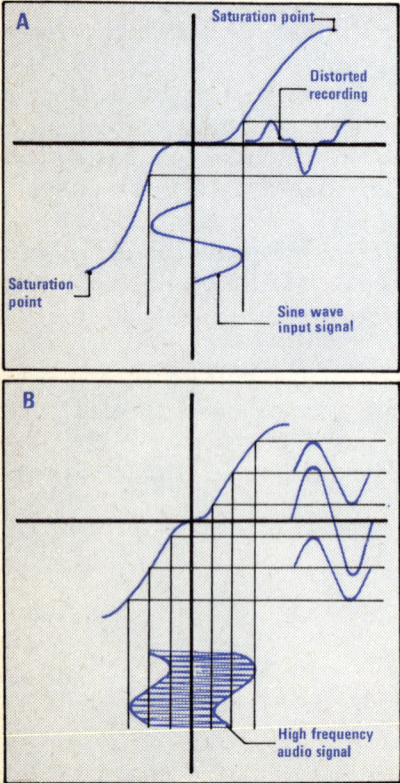

A Curve of the tape transfer characteristic. Note the sharp kink at the origin of the curve and the resultant distortion of the input signal when recorded.
B Distortion is minimised by super-imposing the audio signal on a high frequency bias voltage which offsets the waveform on to the straight part of the characteristic.

although physically aligned (see page 2) have no common magnetic sense. Passing the tape over a concentrated varying magnetic flux gives these minute bar magnets a series of areas of common magnetic polarity. Thus, as we have described, the pattern of particle magnetisation is a replica of the applied electrical signal.

Bias

Unfortunately it is not quite this simple: the applied magnetising force (i.e. the magnetic flux produced by the record head) and the strength of signal recorded on the tape are not directly proportional. This can be seen more easily by referring to the tape transfer curve for a particular tape. The H axis represents the magnetising force and the B axis the magnetic flux induced in the oxide by the flux. It can be seen that at the origin and at the extremes of the curve an increase in magnetising force makes little difference to the degree of magnetisation. However, the central part of the positive and negative sections is virtually a straight line and the resulting magnetic flux is roughly proportional to the magnetising force.

We can see, then, that if a signal swinging symmetrically about the B axis is applied to the tape, the recording will be distorted because of the kink in the transfer curve. To overcome this distortion the input signal has to be offset on to the linear part of the curve. This is done by superimposing the audio signal on to a high frequency (i.e. ultrasonic, and therefore inaudible) bias waveform which gives the necessary offset.

It is important that the bias waveform is itself free from distortion as any lack of symmetry in the bias envelope will result in distortion of the audio signal. Iron oxide and CrO_2 tapes vary widely in their bias requirements, as much as 40% more bias voltage being required for chrome tape.

The foregoing is a brief and much simplified explanation of the recording process. Readers who would like to make a more detailed study of the subject should refer to the books listed in the Appendix. For the present purpose, if we can accept that a tape recording is a means of storing a magnetic analogue of an audio signal, we can now consider the replay system.

Replay

Record and replay heads are basically similar but whereas the front gap of a typical record head, for a machine running at 7½ and 3¾ in/s (19 and 9.5 cm/s), might be 0.000 24 in (6 μm) the replay gap will be of the order of 0.0001 in (2.5μm). As we shall see the width of the gap has a direct bearing on the high frequency performance of the machine and on cassette recorders this gap may be as little as 0.000 04 in (1 μm). Because the replay head tolerances are so tight, if a dual purpose (i.e. record/replay) head is constructed it will to all intents and purposes be a replay head, although a compromise gap width will be used which is rather wider than would be used for a replay-only head.

In order accurately to recover the signal from the tape it must cross the replay head at exactly the same speed and in the same direction as for the original recording. However, on this occasion instead of an electrical signal energising the head winding, the energy is provided by the stored magnetic pattern on the tape. What happens is that the N and S poles on the tape produce a flux which emerges from the surface of the tape and completes the magnetic circuit through the air. As the tape crosses the head, the flux is offered a path through the head core which is several thousand times easier than the path through air.

We have seen that when a material is magnetised a field, or flux, is created, this flux completing a circuit from the north pole to the south. If a coil of wire is wound around the magnetic material, the flux due to the initial magnetisation will produce a voltage across the ends of the wire. If the magnetic effect is removed from the material the flux will instantaneously collapse and this collapse will also produce a voltage across the coil. The significant fact to note is that a voltage is produced by changing flux, regardless of whether that flux is a developing or a collapsing one. The more rapidly the flux is changing, whether in a negative or a positive sense, the greater will be the voltage produced.

Relating this to the magnetised tape we can see that as it crosses the replay head the succeeding N-to-S and S-to-N 'magnets' will produce an alternating magnetic flux, resulting in an alternating output voltage from the head winding. The frequency of the voltage will be identical to that of the original audio input signal. To this extent the replay process is somewhat simpler than the recording process, and it would appear that if one amplified the output from the head and fed it to a loudspeaker, all would be well.

It is not quite that easy because, as we have just said, the more rapid the rate of change of flux the greater the output from the head. In terms of the tape recording, low frequency signals produce long magnets and high frequency signals produce short magnets. Therefore a frequency of 2000 Hz (1 Hz equals 1 cycle per second) will produce magnets half the length of those produced by a 1000 Hz signal. When replayed, the 2000 Hz recording will induce a varying flux in the head which is changing at twice the rate of the flux due to the 1000 Hz recording: the result is that the output from the head doubles as the frequency doubles. Doubling the frequency is the same as raising the pitch by an octave: doubling the voltage is the same as increasing it by 6 decibels (dB). Which is why it is usually stated that the output from an ideal replay head rises at 6 dB/octave.

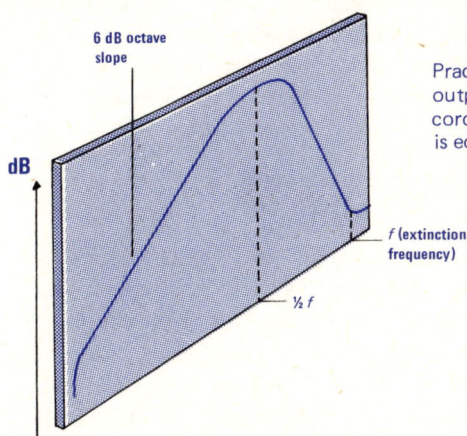

6 dB octave slope

dB

Practical response of the replay head. The output of the head is zero when the recorded wavelength (i.e. two bar magnets) is equal to the effective head gap.

f (extinction frequency)

½ f

In practice, this response is not realised, with head losses causing high frequency roll-off. From a practical point of view, the most serious loss occurs at the point when the recorded wavelength (i.e. two bar magnets) is equal to the effective gap of the replay head. When this point is reached, the variation of flux occurs within the gap, consequently there is no flux linkage with the core and hence no output. The replay head therefore determines the highest frequency which can be reproduced and it should have the narrowest practical gap.

Tape speed is, naturally, a significant factor in frequency response because as the tape speed increases so the recorded magnets become proportionately longer, making a number of the parameters less critical. For creative work a tape speed of 7½ in/s (19 cm/s) makes a sensible compromise between good audio quality and reasonable tape economy.

To compensate for the 6 dB/octave rise in output followed by the roll-off as the extinction frequency is approached, an equalising amplifier is used so that when the tape is replayed an almost level output is obtained over a large part of the audio spectrum. On many recorders it is possible to switch the meter to read the equalised off-tape signal, so that it may be monitored visually as well as by ear.

The final part of the electronics system concerned with signal processing is the output amplifier. Frequently machines are supplied in a form referred to as a *tape deck*. In this case the recorder will not have a power output stage and the final amplifier will simply be a buffer providing a headphone feed plus an output of the order of 1 V for an external amplifier. For creative work, particularly on location, a version which incorporates power amplifiers and loudspeakers can be useful for monitoring purposes, but this will be heavier and more expensive.

The Tape Transport System

We have now briefly outlined the recording and replay operations and the various electronic modules have been explained. Equally important is the means by which the tape is transported and this calls for engineering of a high order. The requirements of the tape transport system are that the tape shall be moved at constant speed, that it shall be maintained under constant tension, that the take-up of the tape shall be smooth and free from snatch when the machine is started, and that the tape is maintained in intimate contact with the heads. Additionally, it must be possible to spool the tape in either direction at high speed without damage and there must be an effective braking system, capable of stopping the tape quickly from any speed. During fast-winding operations, to avoid excessive head wear, a lift mechanism should hold the tape clear of the head faces.

Three Motors

There are several ways in which the drive systems—capstan, feed spool and take-up spool—can be operated. The simplest and most expensive, and probably the best, is to fit three independent

Basic tape deck showing main components.

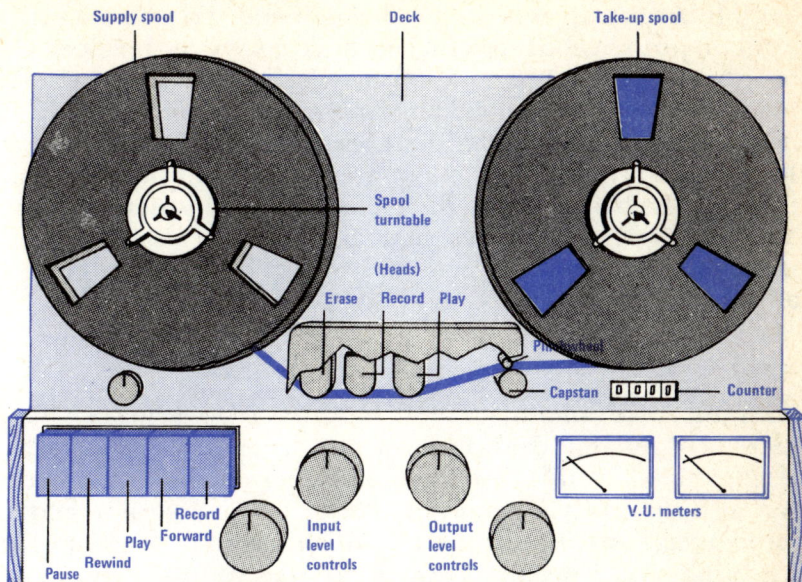

Supply spool   Deck   Take-up spool

Spool turntable

(Heads)

Erase   Record   Play

Pinchwheel

Capstan   Counter

Record   Forward   Input level controls   Output level controls   V.U. meters

Play

Pause   Rewind

motors. The first then drives the capstan (the tape, of course, being moved by being rolled under pressure between the pinch wheel and capstan) whilst the other two drive the supply and take-up turntables. Usually, during play and record, the supply and take-up motors are operated at a fraction of their full voltage, so that they do little more than apply tension to the tape. The supply motor is designed to run clockwise whilst the take-up motor runs anticlockwise. During play and record the supply motor tries to run clockwise but the tape under the capstan drive is constantly being drawn from the feed spool against this back tension.

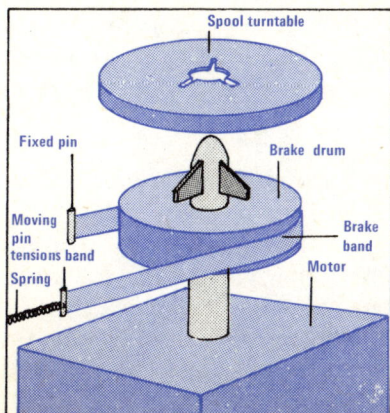

Spool turntable

Fixed pin

Brake drum

Moving pin tensions band

Brake band

Motor

Spring

A typical braking system in which the spool turntable is retarded by a wrap-round band tensioned by a spring.

11

In the fast-wind mode the full voltage is supplied to one motor (supply or take-up) whilst the other is operated at reduced voltage to maintain tension. An efficient braking system is essential: it must stop both reels simultaneously but gently so that the tape neither spills nor stretches. The most common consists of a drum driven by each spool motor shaft, around which is fitted a friction band (page 11). When the brakes are applied a spring or solenoid tensions the bands which then wrap tightly around the drums. The switch which actuates the braking system also removes the power from the motors and, provided the brakes are correctly adjusted, the tape comes smoothly to a standstill.

Single Motor

A number of manufacturers have succeeded in producing extremely reliable deck mechanisms which are powered by a single motor. In this case the motor not only drives the capstan but also indirectly supplies the power for tape tension and fast wind operations. A typical deck will have belts or friction wheels coupling the capstan flywheel to the supply and take-up turntables, and in play and record a slipping clutch system applies the necessary tension to the tape. In fast-wind the drive ratio to the winding reel is stepped up and the clutch is locked, thus producing a rapid tape wind. Although this system is very effective it does tend to require more maintenance than the three-motor type of deck.

Capstan Motor & Speed Control

The drive capstan is a precision ground shaft which may either be a straight extension of the motor shaft (direct drive) or an extension of the spindle of a heavy and accurately balanced flywheel (indirect drive). In the latter case the capstan motor drives the flywheel via a belt or idler wheel. Most three-motor decks have a directly driven capstan and most single-motor decks employ indirect drive.

In order to obtain a selection of tape speeds it is necessary to be able to change the rotational speed of the capstan. This can be done by changing the speed of the motor itself or by using a stepped pulley system, similar to that used for changing the speed of a record turntable, to reduce or increase the ratio between the drive motor and the capstan. The second method needs no explanation but the first method, varying the motor speed, can be applied in several ways.

Until recently most directly driven capstans were powered by a synchronous motor (i.e. one in which the speed of rotation is proportional to the supply frequency). The speed of such a motor can be determined from the formula:

$$S = 120f/N$$

where f = Supply frequency
N = Number of motor poles
S = Motor speed in rev/min.

For example on a 50 Hz supply an eight-pole motor will revolve at 750 rev/min. Halving the number of poles will double the speed, doubling the number will halve the speed. Therefore the simplest method of changing the tape speed is to switch additional sets of poles in or out of circuit.

An alternative approach and one which has become more practical with the advent of solid state circuits and miniature components, is to use a servo-control system. In this method a d.c. capstan motor is used, the speed of which varies with the applied voltage: an electronic motor control circuit then senses the motor speed and compensates for any deviation by varying the supply voltage.

A and B show how this principle can be applied. In A a regulated power supply feeds a reference voltage to a comparator and the output of the comparator drives the capstan motor. A magnetic

Block diagram showing two of the principal methods of electronic motor control. A, voltage control, and B, frequency control.

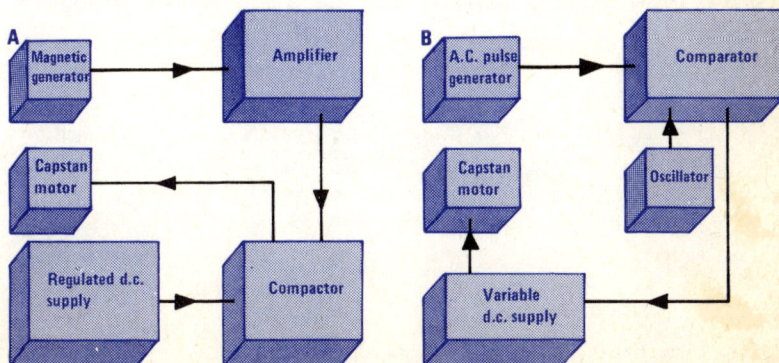

generator driven by the capstan motor produces a voltage which varies with the speed of the motor and this voltage is fed to the second input of the comparator. Any difference between the reference voltage and that from the magnetic generator causes the output voltage of the comparator to vary sufficiently to correct the motor speed.

In B a stable oscillator is used for a reference: the d.c. motor supply is variable and is controlled by the signal from the comparator. A magnetic pick-up head produces a series of pulses by induction from a toothed, rotating ring concentric with the capstan. The pulse frequency is compared with the oscillator frequency and any difference again produces an error signal from the comparator which varies the d.c. supply to the motor.

A further refinement of this type of servo-control is to use a synchronous motor but to drive it from an oscillator within the tape recorder rather than from the mains*. A comparator circuit then senses the motor speed and varies the frequency of the internal oscillator to which the motor is locked, to correct any speed error. This type of system is known as a *phase-locked loop* and is the most expensive and most stable form of motor control.

Extremely good results can be achieved both with synchronous and with electronically regulated motors. Quite minor speed variations of the tape manifest themselves as *wow and flutter*, which is a periodic variation of pitch, particularly noticeable on continuous tones and held notes. For this reason the capstan must not only rotate at constant speed, but must be precision ground and accurately aligned. In fact the mechanical quality and tolerances of the tape transport components are as important to the overall performance of the machine as is the design of the electronic modules—a fact which seems frequently to be overlooked.

*Or supply voltage.

2. Choosing a suitable machine

Two basic formats are at present in use for domestic audio tape recording: the cassette system, based on ⅛ in (3.12 mm) tape, and the open reel system, based on ¼ in (6.25 mm) tape. In almost all creative work some editing is required and it is important that this can be accomplished quickly and with precision. For this reason, and for other technical reasons which will become clear later, the cassette machine is of limited use to the recording enthusiast. Its main applications, apart from the obvious one of replaying prerecorded music, are as an audio notebook and as a convenient means of recording effects on location. Any material collected on the cassette will have to be copied, possibly with subsequent editing, to an open reel tape. Because of the limitations of the cassette machine for creative work, we will confine ourselves in the main to discussing open reel machines.

The merit of the open reel machine, then, is flexibility, and the art of choosing a recorder is to find a model which has all the facilities one requires and none one does not. As this is practically impossible, some compromises must be made and the choice narrowed down to three or four models, each with their own good and bad features.

Remember that the most expensive and most complex machine is not necessarily the best suited to your purpose. The first thing, therefore, is to be objective and to decide if this is an all-consuming hobby or whether you simply want to make an odd recording with the kids. In the latter case a two-speed machine, taking 5 in (12.5 cm) spools, running at 3¾ and 7½ in/s (9.5 and 19 cm/s) and having limited input facilities, would be adequate. As soon as anything more ambitious is tackled the cost of the machine, and the ancillary equipment required, multiplies at an alarming rate, which is why it is important to define one's objectives.

A good open reel recorder is essential for creative work. The absolute minimum requirements, say for home recordings with the children, are: speeds 3.75 and 7.5 in/s (9.5 and 19 cm/s); 12.5 cm spool capacity; mic and radio inputs.

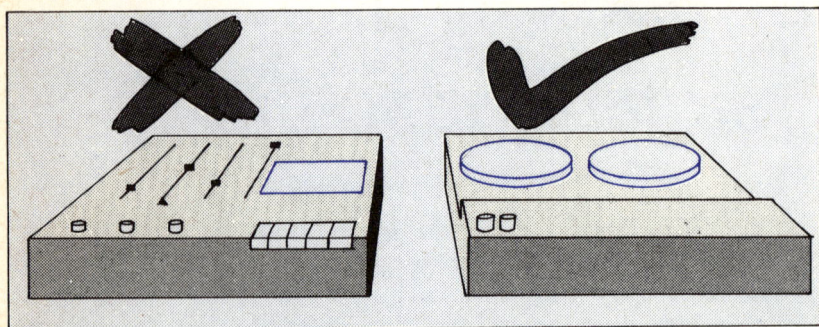

If recording is to be a major hobby, absorbing both time and capital, then a reputable workhorse of a machine is required. One which will not depreciate too quickly or need constant attention but at the same time has a good performance and the right 'feel'. Ergonomic design is important in tape recording because a great deal depends on the manual dexterity of the operator: frequently used controls should come easily to hand and function simply with a minimum of physical effort.

Later in this chapter we will endeavour to explain the various terms used in specifying the performance of a machine; we will also indicate the minimum standards one should expect from a machine intended for creative work. Before this, though, it is worth taking a more general look at the main features of a recorder so that we can begin to form an impression of the machine which will suit our purpose.

Leads

A browse through the advertising pages of hi-fi journals will reveal that the men who publicise tape recorders know very little of their practical operation. In almost all illustrations the seductively illuminated recorder will be shown with the deck standing vertically; invariably there will be an absence of mains leads and connecting cables. Both these points are of crucial

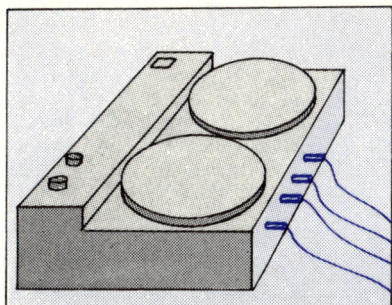

The machine must be designed primarily for horizontal operation with good access to the input and output sockets. Ideally the mains lead will be detachable.

importance to the practical man: it is absolutely essential that the deck is primarily designed for horizontal operation, with controls logically arranged and easily accessible to someone sitting in front of it, and that the cables can be connected without difficulty. The reasons one rarely sees connecting cables in advertisements are firstly that they make the picture look untidy, and secondly that the input and output sockets are frequently so placed that leads cannot be re-plugged without standing the machine on end.

The mains lead may be of the captive type or it may plug into a socket on the machine. All other things being equal, the machine with a detachable lead is a better bet; it packs away more easily, and is less trouble to transport, than one with a trailing cable. There is also less likelihood of falling downstairs with it and severely damaging both parties!

Motors

In the first chapter it was mentioned that a deck may have a single motor which drives the spools and the capstan, or it may have separate motors for spooling and for capstan drive. At the lower end of the price spectrum, there is not a great deal of choice—most machines have a single motor. Amongst the more complex domestic, and the semi-professional, machines, the single-motor deck is more rare and, in general, its tape transport system is inferior to that of the three-motor deck. The three-motor system tends to have a smoother and better controlled fast-wind, the initial take-up on playback is less prone to bounce erratically as

17

the tape spills rapidly from the capstan, and the speed consistency of the tape drive, both long and short term, is more accurate.

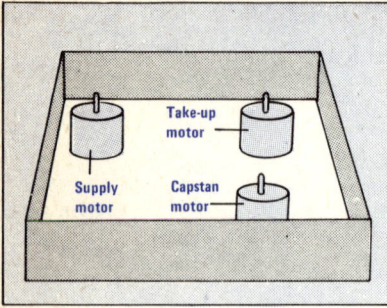

All things being equal, the three-motor deck is superior in terms of operational convenience and long term reliability. Where cost is an important factor the choice will probably have to be confined to single-motor machines, but a number of these do have very good performance figures.

As far as servicing and long-term reliability are concerned, the three-motor deck is preferable as it is mechanically less complex and requires little attention apart from occasional adjustment of the brakes and the odd drop of oil. The single-motor deck, with a multitude of mechanical linkages, drive belts, friction wheels and clutches, has a lower initial cost and is frequently very reliable, but the wear and tear on the components and the necessity for maintaining accurate torques and spring pressures, mean that more regular maintenance is required. These adjustments are not complex but they can be time consuming, making service rather expensive unless the owner is well equipped and able to do it for himself. Again, much depends on the use to which the machine will be put, and for many purposes, where prolonged heavy duty is not involved, the single-motor deck will be satisfactory.

Another important consideration is the ease with which the tape can be threaded through the head block and looped around the associated tape guides. A lengthy editing session, when spools are constantly being juggled around as sequences are assembled from several tapes. can be a nightmare on many machines. There is a

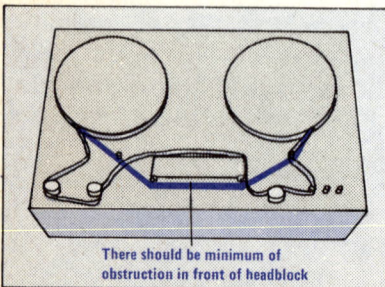

There should be minimum of obstruction in front of headblock

There is a perversity about recording tape which demands that it seek out every available switch, knob, lever or screw to attach itself to and from which it can only be extracted with the greatest difficulty.

perversity about recording tape which demands that it seek out every available switch, knob, lever or screw to attach itself to and from which it can only be extracted with the greatest difficulty: frequently this results in creasing or other physical damage to the tape. For editing, the simpler the deck layout the better, and there should be a minimum of obstructions in front of the head block.

Pressure Pads

A major frustration and hindrance in editing is caused by the pressure pad. It consists of a small piece of felt, or similar material, attached to a spring loaded arm and its purpose, as the name suggests, is to apply pressure to the tape. The pad is only operative during recording and playback, when it presses the tape

Pressure pads are a mixed blessing: they can cause rapid head wear and make editing difficult. On the credit side, they do ensure that the tape makes good contact with the heads.

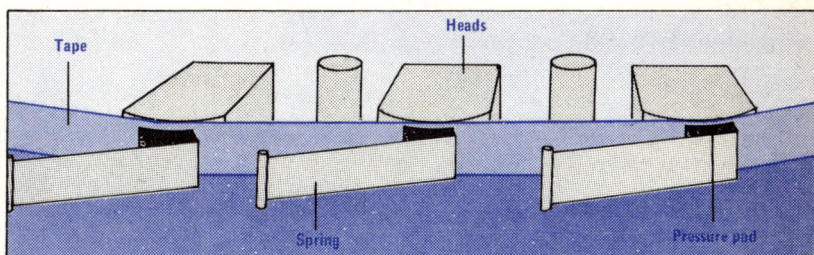

against the tape head, maintaining it in intimate contact with the face of the head. Some machines have just a single pad, on either the record or playback head; more commonly if pads are used they are fitted to all heads. They are good in that they ensure that vital head-to-tape contact is obtained, but they can cause rapid head wear and produce an unpleasant scrape as the tape backing rubs against the pad.

A better approach, but one calling for considerable electrical and mechanical precision, is to arrange the tape path so that the arc of the heads combined with the back tension and natural 'wrap round' of the tape is sufficient to give the required head-to-tape contact. For the enthusiast the question of pressure pads is an important one: it is cheaper to manufacture and easier to engineer a deck using pressure pads, but without them editing, particularly accurate marking of the tape, is much simplified, as we shall see 19 in Chapter 9. It is important to note that it is seldom possible successfully to remove pads from a machine which is designed to operate with them, so it is important to make the correct decision in the first place.

Spool Size

Until recently very few machines of the domestic type would accept spools of larger diameter than 7 in (18 cm): in professional circles the standard spool size was 10½ in (27 cm). As the gap between professional and domestic standards narrowed, so a number of domestic tape decks appeared, capable of accepting larger spools, including the 10½ in (27 cm). The smaller spools are generally made from plastics, they have a small centre hole and are frequently described as *cine* spools, as they conform to the standards for 8 mm film projection. The larger spools are usually made from aluminium, they have a large centre hole for which a special adaptor is required to fit them on to a cine hub, and they are known as NAB spools. NAB stands for the National Association of Broadcasters, an American institute which originated the standard for this type of spool.

Larger spools give a longer playing time for a given tape speed, without changing tape: they are also far easier to manipulate when editing.

A 10½ in (27 cm) spool with cine centre.
B 10½ in (27 cm) spool with NAB centre.
C 7 in (18 cm) spool with cine centre.
D Adaptor for type B spool when used with cine hub.

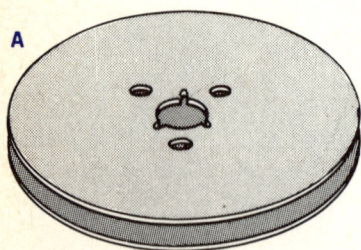

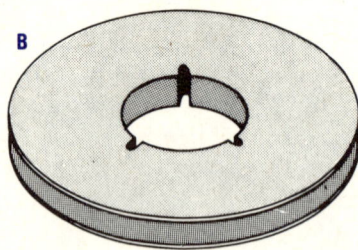

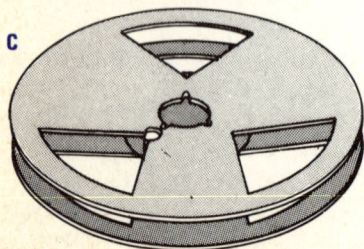

In practical terms there are two major advantages to using large spools: firstly, for a given tape speed a longer playing time can be obtained without changing tape, and, secondly, the larger spools are far easier to manipulate when editing. It is safe to say that anyone who intends to become seriously involved with editing should opt for a deck which will accept 10½in (27cm) spools. If it is too much of a financial burden to buy tape in professional lengths, it is well worth keeping a pair of empty 10½in spools and transferring the tape to these for editing purposes.

Tape Speed

Associated with the decision regarding spool size is the matter of tape speed and here two conflicting requirements have to be considered. The slower the speed the greater the tape economy; the higher the speed the better the recording quality. For serious work no speed below 3¾in/s (9.5cm/s) need be considered, and this should be reserved for speech recording, and no speed above 15in/s (38cm/s) is practicable.

Some machines have three speeds and these may be 1⅞, 3¾ and 7½in/s (4.75, 9.5 and 19cm/s) or 3¾, 7½ and 15in/s (9.5, 19 and 38cm/s); others have two speeds 1⅞/3¾ (4.75/9.5), 3¾/7½ (9.5/19) or 7½/15 (19/38). If a three-speed deck is chosen, the more useful all-round machine is the higher speed version; if a two-speed deck is chosen the 3¾ and 7½in/s (9.5 and 19cm/s) version is more useful. For most amateur applications the 7½in/s (19cm/s) speed will be found to give the best compromise between cost, quality and ease of editing.

Controls

The tape transport system and the related functions of play, record and fast-wind may be controlled either directly by manually operated switches or indirectly by means of relays, solenoids or electronic switching circuits. Manual control has the merit of simplicity but it tends to be more sluggish and cannot readily be remote controlled. It requires a certain amount of physical effort, giving a heavy feel to the controls, is less precise in operation and depends for satisfactory operation on the accurate adjustment of a number of mechanical linkages. Electronic control is positive; it has a lightness of touch and the deck can be switched rapidly from one function to another. On some machines the deck switching is controlled by a logic circuit which 21 acts as a memory and if, for instance, play is selected whilst fast-winding, the tape will stop and then automatically begin to play back. This type of system can easily be remotely controlled: a cable is plugged in, the far end of which has a switch panel which duplicates some of the deck switches. Electronic control is more expensive than manual but it is operationally more convenient and less tiring to use for editing.

Spooling Performance

Fast-winding on most decks is accomplished either by energising the appropriate spool motor or by an indirect drive from the capstan motor: spooling therefore tends to be at a fixed speed. On some machines, where the drive system is under-powered, it will be found that the tape slows down as the spool fills up, because the motor cannot cope with the load. To check the spooling performance of a deck, load a full spool of tape, spool it through

A. To check forward wind, load largest possible spools fully loaded with standard play tape. Spool forward until the right-hand reel is almost full. Stop tape, then continue winding. Check that the tape winds off satisfactorily at a reasonable speed. B. To check the rewind performance, make the above test but start off with the full reel on the right and rewind it.

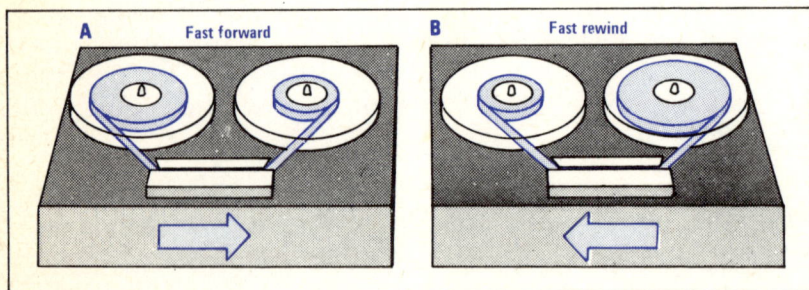

A   Fast forward   B   Fast rewind

almost to the end and stop the machine. Now select fast-wind again and see if the spool motor picks up a reasonable speed with an almost full take-up spool. After this, rewind the tape almost to the beginning, stop it and then check that it will wind off satisfactorily. If you are thinking of buying a recorder with 10½ in (27 cm) spool capacity, be sure to try it out with the large metal spools fully loaded: the weight of 2400 ft (731 m) of standard play tape is considerable.

SWINDON BOOK CO., LTD.

Professional & Medical Book Service

Ocean Centre Branch
346, Ocean Centre, 3/F Kowloon
Tel. 3-670983. 3-692966

M ....

CASH SALE

Date, ... **23 OCT 1979**

Quaht.	Description	@ Price	Amount
1	Martin Creative Tape Recording (New. Technical)	30,00	30,00
		TOTAL $	

SOLD BY

OC № 101697

ALL GOODS SOLD ARE NOT RETURNABLE

Many decks which will accept the large spools are modifications of models originally designed for 7 in (18 cm) spools and simply cannot cope with the additional mass of tape and spool. Some three-motor decks have a single knob for controlling fast-wind: this knob operates a high wattage variable resistor and the supply voltage feed to the spool motors is routed through the variable control. The voltage to either wind motor can therefore be varied over a wide range, giving precise control over the speed of spooling. This facility can be extremely useful for finding a particular part of a tape quickly, provided the tape can be monitored whilst spooling. Two precautions should be observed here: the first is that the tape must be lifted clear of the heads when winding (this should happen automatically, but if not the deck

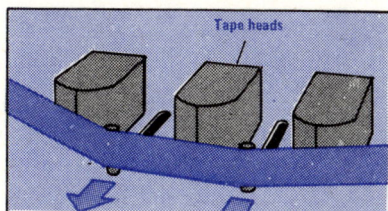

When spooling, (a) ensure that the tape is lifted clear of the heads by the tape guides or some system of moving pins, (b) always monitor a low level whilst spooling, otherwise the high frequency loudspeaker unit may be damaged.

must be modified), otherwise head wear will be excessive: the second is that when monitoring at high speed the loudspeaker level should be reduced as all frequencies are increased in pitch and the additional energy at high frequencies could well destroy the tweeter unit.

Tape Heads

Ideally the machine will have three tape heads—erase, record and replay (page 24). Each can be engineered for a specific purpose, and it is possible to monitor the off-tape signal a fraction of a second after recording. This has two advantages—one can check that the machine is recording satisfactorily, and one can also switch between the incoming and the off-tape signal (known as an A/B test). The importance of an A/B test is that it reveals losses of quality which might otherwise not be noticed at the time. This is because the ear has a relatively short memory for sound quality and level and it is virtually impossible to make a subjective assessment of absolute quality. This is apparent when evaluating loudspeakers: unless an immediate reference is available, say a monitor speaker or the live sound itself, it is very difficult to place three similar loudspeakers in order of merit, as the ear will quickly adapt itself to each sound source. The A/B test is therefore essential for comparing the incoming and the recorded signals, as any quality which is lost at the recording stage cannot be recovered later.

If a machine has three heads the recorded signal can be monitored immediately after recording. The tape crosses heads 1, 2 and 3 in sequence and by throwing a switch (A/B) the incoming signal (A) can be compared with the off-tape signal (B).

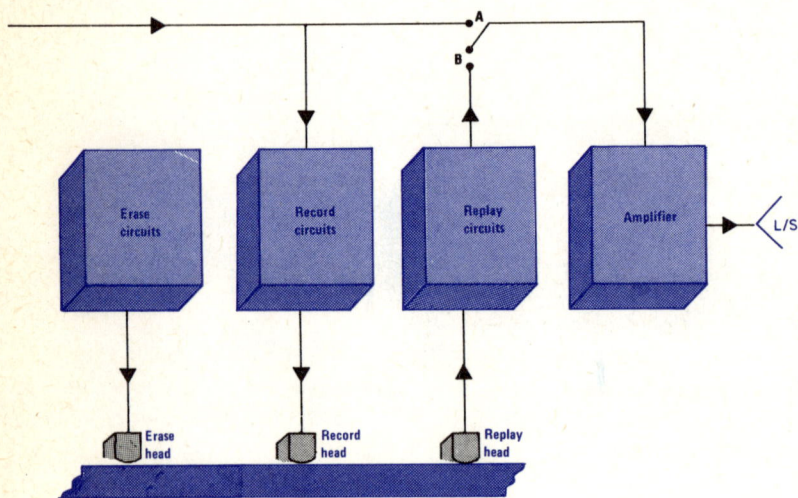

Track Configurations

On the subject of quality, there is a choice of track configurations available and one has to arrive at a sensible compromise between tape economy and recording quality. Remember that if a tape is to be edited it will only be possible to record on one track in any case, unless the tape is copied and the copy edited. For ¼ in (6.25 mm) tape there are several possible track configurations: full track, half-track mono, half-track stereo, quarter-track mono and quarter-track stereo. Additionally on a few recorders it is possible to record multitrack fashion on four separate, parallel tracks. According to requirements each track can then be fed with the same or with different sources.

24

Track configurations. A is the most useful for creative and high fidelity work. B and D are unsatisfactory because the edge tracks are very narrow and liable to curl or to suffer other physical damage during handling. E is not economic. C is satisfactory but more limited in scope than half-track stereo.

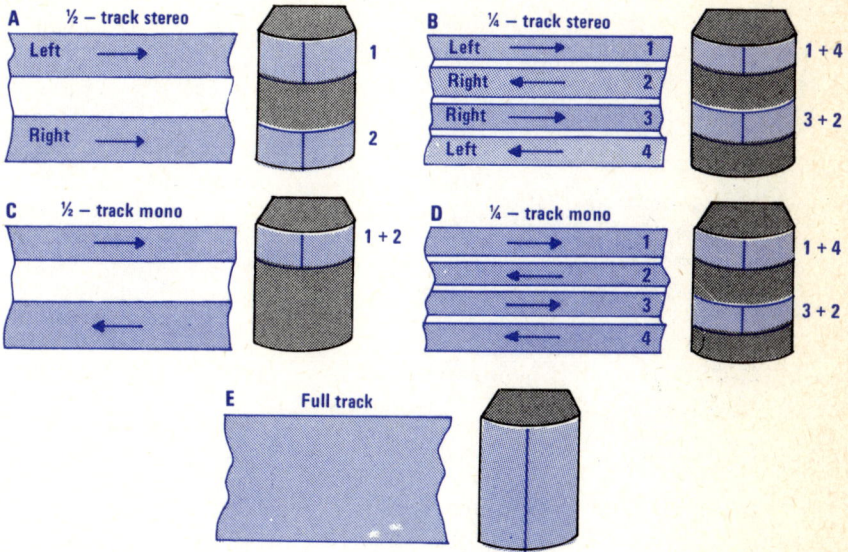

A ½ – track stereo
Left →
Right →
1
2

B ¼ – track stereo
Left →
Right ←
Right →
Left ←
1
2
3
4
1 + 4
3 + 2

C ½ – track mono
→
←
1 + 2

D ¼ – track mono
→
←
→
←
1
2
3
4
1 + 4
3 + 2

E Full track

We can immediately eliminate some of these track systems: full-track recording is prohibitively expensive for the amateur and quarter-track has too many disadvantages for creative work—it gives inferior quality and the edge tracks are liable to curl or to suffer other physical damage during handling. This narrows the choice down to half-track mono or stereo or to a genuine four-track recorder. The machine with four parallel, synchronous tracks is a very different animal from the standard quarter-track recorder and is a wonderful tool for anyone who is keen on music recording; but, again, it is expensive and probably out of reach of most amateur enthusiasts.

We are left with half-track, and as a mono recorder is not a great deal cheaper than a stereo one, it would not be an economic purchase for the enthusiast. The stereo machine is not only more versatile, and offers much more scope to the recordist, but also it can effectively be used as a full-track recorder or for half-track mono, simply by throwing a switch.

25

Input and Output Connections

There are two types of connector in general use: one is in the form of a central pin with an earthed body; the other consists of a standard barrel which may be fitted with one of a number of multi-pin plug inserts. The first is frequently described as an RCA *phono* plug, although it is now made by many other manufacturers; the second is known as a DIN plug, D.I.N. being the initial letters of the German standards organisation which recommended this design.

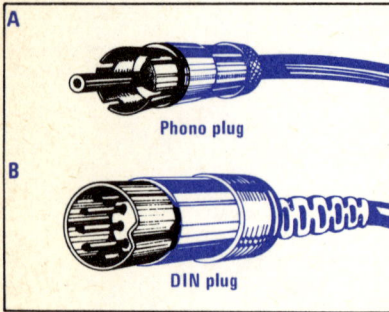

Types of connector. A, phono. B, DIN.

It is apparent from the nature of the two designs that when a phono system is used an individual connection is required for each input and output of each channel. With a DIN plug a multicore cable is used and several circuits can be connected using a single lead. On the face of it, the DIN-based system is superior; it is easier to use and to connect and, in theory, when two items of equipment conforming to DIN standards are linked together, the input and output levels should match satisfactorily. In practice this is not always so and one will still find some manufacturers who use DIN connectors but do not conform to the DIN standards. Occasionally one will find that the standard pin connections are not adhered to. The phono-based system requires a considerable harness of cable in a complex recording set-up; on the other hand because each connection is individually made, the phono system has an in-built flexibility which is lacking with DIN connectors.

Most of the considerations affecting the purchase of a tape recorder for creative work have now been discussed. We take it for granted that a machine which meets the earlier criteria will have an accurate meter for indicating recording level. The techniques of mixing and of level control are discussed in Chapters 4, 6, 7 and 8.

Specifications

In a book of this type there is not space to deal exhaustively with specifications. It will be worthwhile, however, to indicate the sort of figures one should look for in a good quality open reel recorder. In the remainder of this chapter we will briefly define the various parameters of performance and quote figures which are typical of a good all round performance. Firstly, however, we must say a few words about the much abused and little understood *decibel*.

The decibel is a ratio. As its name suggests its value is one tenth of a *bel*, the bel being too large a unit for practical use. For those with a mathematical interest in the subject, the decibel is a logarithmic unit and when expressing the relationship of two sound waves in terms of their relative power, the expression $N(dB) = 10\log_{10}(W_2/W_1)$ is used, where W_2 and W_1 are the two powers concerned. Because decibel measurements are based on ratios, the reference level must either be implicit or stated. In acoustic measurements, the reference used is the threshold of hearing which is 0.0002 dyne/cm² or 0.0002 microbar (μbar). The dynamic range of human hearing is approximately 120 dB from the threshold of hearing to the threshold of pain.

When comparing pressures, rather than powers, the expression $N(dB) = 20\log_{10}(P_2/P_1)$ is used. The decibel is a particularly useful method of expressing values in audio work because the ear responds logarithmically to changes in sound intensity—1 dB being the minimum change of intensity that the ear can detect on a continuous signal. To give an example, if we compare the sound intensity produced by 200 motor bikes with that produced by 100; if we apply the above formula we find that $N(dB) = 20\log_{10}(200/100)$ or $20\log_{10}2$ which, surprisingly, is only 6 dB. So next time 200 motor bikes come roaring up your road, comfort yourself with the thought that they are only 6 dB louder than half that number.

Whereas doubling the pressure or voltage is equivalent to an increase of 6 dB, doubling the power is equivalent to an increase of 3 dB. Decibels are also used to represent ratios of power, voltage and current in electrical circuits. Readers who would like to study the decibel in greater detail should refer to one of the many books on this subject*.

We have now outlined the application of the decibel to acoustic and electrical measurement, and it must be stressed again that the

*See Gordon J. King, *The Audio Handbook*, Newnes-Butterworths (1975).

important thing to remember is that a reference level must be understood or given for the figure to have any meaning. This will be seen more clearly as we discuss the specification parameters below. All the figures given apply to a good quality open reel recorder running at 7½in/s (19 cm/s).

Wow & Flutter

This is an expression used to describe short-term speed variations which produce a rhythmic wavering of pitch on the recording. It is particularly noticeable on sustained notes, such as in piano music. Where this variation of pitch is at a rate of less than about twenty times a second it is called *wow* and when the variation is more rapid it is called *flutter*. Because the effect of wow and flutter is subjectively more annoying at some rates than at others, the measuring instrument usually incorporates a weighting network so that the read-out takes account of the subjective effect. The measurement is made using a constant tone at 3150 Hz (this is the ear's most sensitive region) and the reading indicates the percentage short-term speed variation. The standard measurement, according to DIN 45:509, should be the maximum speed variation resulting from recording and subsequent playback on the same machine. The maximum or peak reading is less flattering than an averaging, or r.m.s., reading and many manufacturers still quote weighted r.m.s. figures. One would

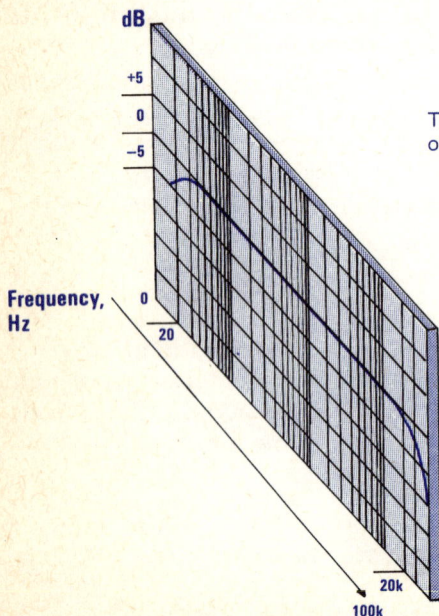

The ideal tape recorder has a flat response over the entire audio spectrum.

expect the specification for wow and flutter to be ± 0.08%, peak weighted, or about 0.06% weighted r.m.s. One should not accept a machine with a figure of worse than ± 0.1%, peak weighted.

Frequency Response

This indicates the portion of the audio spectrum over which the machine has a reasonably level response. In other words all frequencies recorded at a given level will reproduce at that level. The response of an ideal recorder is a straight line. In practice there is always some deviation from the ideal, although with a good recorder the deviation will be confined to the extremes of the audio spectrum. It is customary to specify the limits of the response at a particular speed for a given deviation. At 7½in/s(19 cm/s), for instance, this might be 30 Hz to 18 kHz +2/-3 dB. The maximum positive deviation is 2 dB from the datum line and the maximum negative deviation is 3 dB. This is a good performance but what is significant is not so much the extent of the deviation, so long as it does not exceed about 3 dB, but the smoothness of the curve. Because the record amplifier has a high frequency boost circuit, it is customary for frequency response measurements to be made at low level to avoid tape overload at high frequencies. The reference level used is normally 20 dB below 0 v.u.

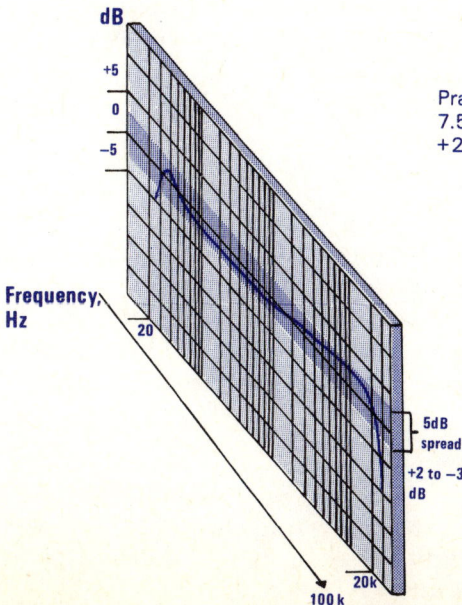

Practical response of a good recorder at 7.5 in/s (19 cm/s): 30 Hz to 18 kHz +2/-3 dB.

29

Distortion

Distortion is largely dependent on the type of tape and on the bias setting, although a number of other electronic design factors are involved. Usually it is measured at 333 Hz at lower tape speeds and at 1000 Hz for speeds of 7½ in/s (19 cm/s) and above. A recording is made at a given level (0v.u. or +3v.u.) and then replayed so that the distortion can be analysed. We would expect a figure of not more than 1.5% at 0v.u. and 2.5% at +3v.u., but we would prefer a figure of 1% or below at 0v.u.

Signal-to-Noise Ratio

Here the manufacturer is expressing the proportion of unwanted random electronic and tape noise produced by his machine, relative to a given record level. A typical figure might be 52 dB, unweighted, at 1 kHz, below 0v.u. This means that relative to the replay output of a tape recorded to 0v.u. (or a standard tape flux may be quoted instead—320 nWb/m) the system noise of machine plus tape is 52 dB below the reference level. So we can see that the figure of 52 dB is meaningless unless that reference is known. Again, because the ear is not equally sensitive to all frequencies, some types of noise are subjectively more annoying than others, and it is customary to have a weighting network in the measuring device. A number of different weighting standards exist and the noise figure can be improved by anything from 4 to about 14 dB according to the test frequency, filter used and the noise characteristic. We would expect an unweighted signal-to-noise (S/N) ratio in the order of 55 dB; weighting will improve this to about 66 dB and noise reduction will give a further selective improvement.

Crosstalk

Usually measured at 1 kHz, this indicates the extent to which material record on one track can break through on to an adjacent track nd produce a very low level output. With a stereo recorder we would expect the crosstalk from a 1 kHz signal recorded to 0v.u. to be around −45 dB for stereo and −60 dB for mono.

Inputs

We would expect the machine to have low impedance (200–600 Ω) and high impedance (above 100 k Ω) microphone inputs for each channel, plus auxiliary and radio.

In this chapter we have discussed in some detail the factors affecting the choice of a machine for creative work, and briefly explained some of the major parameters of the specification. No machine will fully satisfy all the requirements given but you should now be in a position to make a short list.

3. Choice and use of microphones

Later chapters will deal with specific techniques for music, drama and documentary recording but we must now consider microphones in some detail. Second only to the recorder itself, the choice of the correct microphone for a particular application is the most important decision the recordist has to make. Whereas with a tape recorder choice is limited partly by common sense considerations of price and flexibility, and partly by factors of physical and electronic design, with a microphone there is a much more elusive problem. Certainly its specification will give certain basic information about its performance, but it will tell nothing of its 'sound' or the way in which it should be used.

This problem of subjective sound quality also applies to an extent when choosing pickups and loudspeakers. Devices such as these, which convert energy from one form to another, are known as *transducers*. Ideally the energy conversion should be so perfect that nothing is added to nor taken from the original sound. With the microphone, acoustic energy in the form of a sound wave is converted to electrical energy; with the pickup, mechanical energy—stored in the form of a modulated groove—is released as the disc rotates and vibrates the stylus, the movement of which produces a voltage proportional to the stylus velocity; with the loudspeaker, a varying electrical input drives a cone which creates a sound wave having the same characteristics as the original input signal.

None of these transducer systems is perfect and the original signal is degraded by various forms of distortion. Some of the more common problems are: resonance of the moving element and of its casing and mounting; break-up and overload due to the very large excursions resulting from low frequency signals; unsatisfactory transient (short duration, high frequency) response due to the inertia of the moving element. Not all of these problems apply to all microphones, but in every instance the sound is in some way modified or changed in character, and further degradation results from the acoustics of the recording room.

At least we can evaluate a pickup or loudspeaker by listening to familiar broadcasters and records in our own home to see which gives the best performance under domestic conditions. With a microphone it is more difficult—few of us have a symphony orchestra, a chamber group or a BBC broadcaster on hand and the first chance we have to evaluate a microphone is often during an important recording. We must, therefore, buy on recommendation, on experience with the equipment of others, and on judgement based on the specification and theoretical performance of a microphone. There is little to be gained by lengthy discussion of the physics of microphones. Their operating principles will merely be outlined, as one does not need to know in detail how a microphone works in order to use it well.

Operating Principles

Regardless of operating principle, all microphones have one factor in common—the diaphragm. This is a plate, membrane or ribbon of crystal, plastics, dielectric or metal which is suspended

A sound wave comprises areas of low and high pressure.

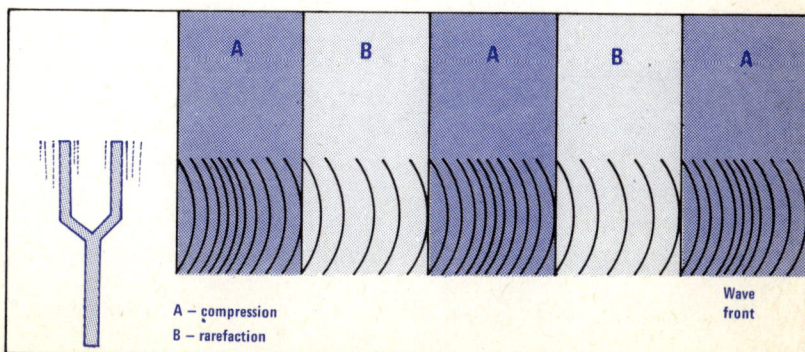

A – compression
B – rarefaction

Wave front

so that it is exposed to sound waves, and caused to vibrate by them. The microphone casing may be such that only one side of the diaphragm is exposed to atmospheric pressure, in which case it will move to and fro about a mean position according to the pressure of the incident sound wave. For instance, a vibrating

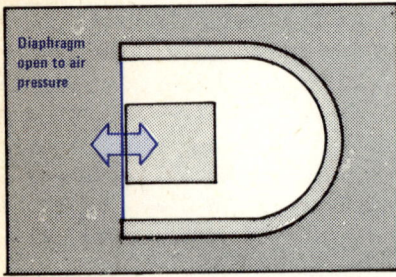

Diaphragm open to air pressure

A 'pressure operated' microphone has one side of the diaphragm totally enclosed.

tuning fork (see page 33) will produce a wave motion in the air, a wave of equally spaced alternate areas of high pressure (compression) and low pressure (rarefaction). At the microphone the compression exerts a force on the diaphragm and depresses it whilst the rarefaction allows it to recover. The effect is an oscillating motion similar to that of the tuning fork. A microphone which operates in this way is of the *pressure operated* family.

Another method of operation uses the *pressure gradient* principle. Here, the diaphragm is exposed on both sides to

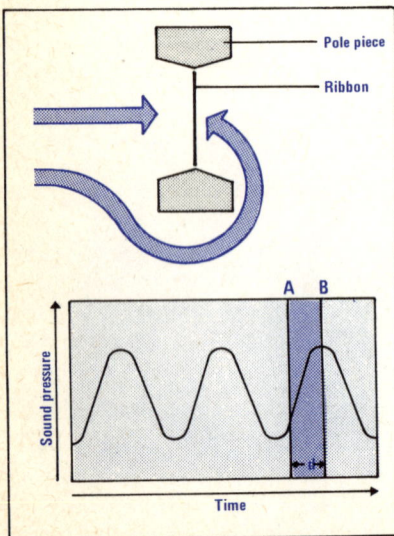

Pole piece

Ribbon

A B

Sound pressure

Time

A 'pressure gradient' microphone has both sides of the diaphragm open to air pressure. The ribbon moves, from moment to moment, towards the area of lower pressure.

atmospheric pressure: it moves not because of pressure on one face but because of the difference in pressure on the two faces. In effect there is a phase (or time) difference in the waves arriving at the front and back of the microphone. As the air pressures are unequal, the diaphragm moves, from instant to instant, towards the area of lower pressure. We shall see later that microphones operating on these two principles have differing characteristics. Also, that by combining the two operating methods within a single microphone the characteristics can be varied.

Types of Microphone

As was said earlier, a microphone is a form of transducer and is usually categorised according to the type of transducer system which is employed. The main types are: *carbon, crystal, ribbon, moving coil* and *capacitor*. We can ignore the carbon microphone as it is a very low quality device and is used mainly in speech communication equipment, e.g. telephone handsets.

Crystal

Crystal microphones are a distinct improvement on the carbon variety; easy to mass produce, they are cheap and have a high output voltage. However, the sound quality is still not good and because the crystal microphone is a high impedance device (we shall discuss this later) it must be used with a relatively short length of cable. This type of microphone should only be used if no other suitable type is available, and its use should be confined to the recording of speech or simple sound effects.

The way in which the crystal microphone works is quite simple. It relies on what is known as the *piezo-electric* effect. If certain

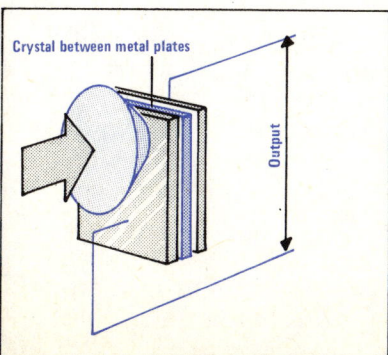

Crystal between metal plates

Output

A crystal microphone has a diaphragm which is coupled to a piezo-electric element. Pressure on the element produces a voltage.

salt crystals (Rochelle is an example) and some types of ceramic material are subjected to mechanical strain, they produce a voltage. This voltage varies according to the pressure applied and the crystal microphone is therefore a pressure-operated device. The crystal or ceramic pickup cartridge is a well known application of this principle and most of us will know from experience that although such pickups perform adequately, they are inferior to the magnetic types. This applies equally to microphones.

Ribbon

Virtually everyone is familiar with the ribbon microphone although he may well not be aware of the fact! For years it has been used by the BBC in talks studios and for continuity announcements. Despite the introduction of other types and more modern designs, the model 4038 ribbon remains one of the finest of all broadcast microphones. It has a quite characteristic sound, particularly noticeable on male voices when used at close working distances. Known technically as bass doubling, the effect is of a rising bass output producing a mellowness of tone often referred to as 'dark brown' when describing speech quality. In the author's mind the ribbon microphone is forever identified with the voice of BBC announcer Frank Phillips (now retired).

The ribbon microphone consists of a horseshoe magnet with a pair of extended pole pieces between which is suspended a thin strip of metal foil. In some designs the foil is corrugated longitudinally for extra strength. The ribbon is clamped top and bottom and leads are connected at either end to carry the output voltage. What happens is that as the metal foil, or ribbon, vibrates it cuts across the magnetic field between the pole pieces, producing a voltage. This effect is well known in physics and whenever a conductor is moved so as to cut across magnetic lines of force, a voltage is produced. If the conductor is wound into a coil more lines of force are cut and a higher voltage is produced. In the case of the ribbon microphone, the moving conductor is also the diaphragm. It is very light and very thin and is thus equivalent to no more than one turn of wire on a coil, so the output voltage is very low. Usually there is a transformer built into the body of the microphone to step up the output.

A ribbon microphone, being a pressure gradient device, depends for its operation on the difference in pressure on the two faces of the diaphragm. The casing is, therefore, perforated at both front

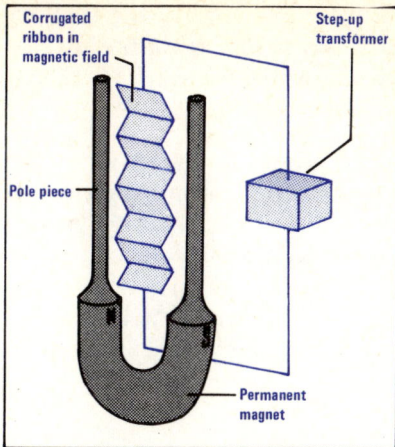

Corrugated
ribbon in
magnetic field

Step-up
transformer

Pole piece

Permanent
magnet

The ribbon microphone operates by having a thin conductor suspended between the pole pieces of a magnet. As the ribbon vibrates it cuts the lines of magnetic force and a voltage is generated.

and back and it is immaterial which of these is used as the 'live' side. Alternatively, both may be used simultaneously. A good ribbon microphone is expensive; it is also fragile, which tends to reduce its suitability for general purpose use. Applications of the various microphones will be discussed later.

Moving Coil

Of the various types of good quality microphone available the recordist is most likely to have encountered the moving coil type, because of its wide range of applications. A typical moving coil microphone consists of a casing which encloses the rear face of the diaphragm and houses a permanent magnet. A coil is coupled, directly or indirectly, to the back of the diaphragm and is positioned between the poles of the magnet. The vibrating diaphragm thus causes the coil to move to and fro within the magnetic field which, as we saw earlier, produces a voltage across

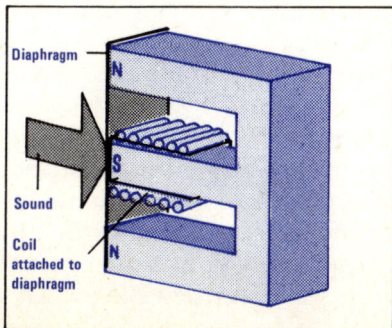

Diaphragm

N

S

Sound

Coil
attached to
diaphragm

N

The moving coil microphone operates on a similar principle to the ribbon but in this case a coil moves in the magnetic field. The coil is coupled to a diaphragm which moves to and fro under the pressure of the incident sound wave.

37

the coil. Because of the number of turns of wire on the coil, the microphone has a higher output than the ribbon and can frequently be used directly to drive an amplifier, without a step-up transformer.

The moving coil device is robust and covers a wide price range, but as a rough guide a good moving coil microphone should be cheaper than a good ribbon. Particularly among lower priced models, it tends to have a rather uneven frequency response, often with a mid to high frequency resonance peak and a transient response which is inferior to the ribbon. Moving coil microphones are pressure operated.

Capacitor

Finally we must consider the capacitor (or condenser) microphone, which is both the most expensive and the most analytical, and is probably the closest approach to the ideal. 'Probably' because the shortcomings of the other microphones

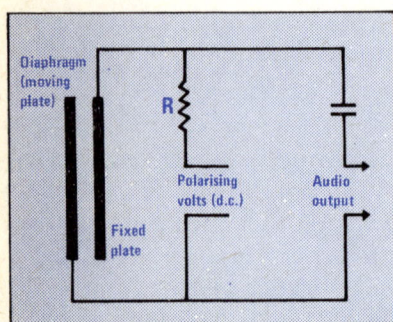

A capacitor microphone requires a polarising voltage which is applied to the plates, one of which is free to move and acts as a diaphragm. Movement of the plate changes the capacitance of the circuit and so causes the current to vary.

can frequently be profitably employed by the creative enthusiast. Unlike all the other types of microphone, the capacitor does not produce its own electromotive force, but requires a source of power. A polarising voltage, say from 25 to 150 Vd.c., is fed to a capacitor through the resistor and the capacitor has one plate which is free to move. This moving plate acts as a diaphragm; it is frequently made from very thin plastics and as it moves it causes the capacitor to change in value, thus varying the current flow in the circuit. A current operated preamplifier in the body of the microphone then steps up the signal and provides an output voltage. A more recent development of this idea, known as the *electret*, uses the capacitor principle, but during manufacture the capacitor is given a form of permanent charge so that an external polarising voltage is not required. The electret microphone has a limited but long life.

Capacitor microphones should be protected from damp, but otherwise are fairly robust and suitable for most purposes. However, for many enthusiasts they are prohibitively expensive. Capacitor microphones are pressure operated.

Polar Diagrams

Before discussing some basic applications for the various types of microphone there is one other characteristic that must be explained: the *polar diagram*. It is represented diagrammatically

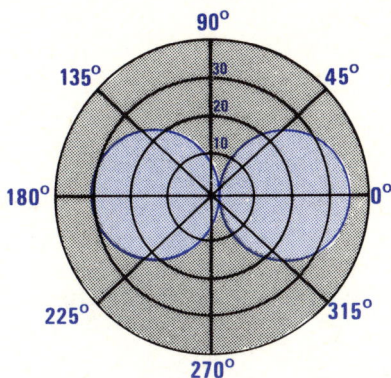

A polar graph shows the relative sensitivity of the microphone to sound waves arriving on and off axis.

on a circular graph with the front of the diaphragm on the 0° radius at the origin of the graph. The polar diagram shows the sensitivity of the microphone to sounds arriving from different angles. The concentric rings on the graph are calibrated in decibels to indicate the off-axis sensitivity to a given signal, relative to the sensitivity on-axis. When the response is plotted it falls into one of three categories—*omnidirectional, cardioid* or *figure-of-eight*—although there are variations in the shape of the

The three main polar diagrams are: 'omni-directional', 'cardioid' and 'figure-of-eight'.

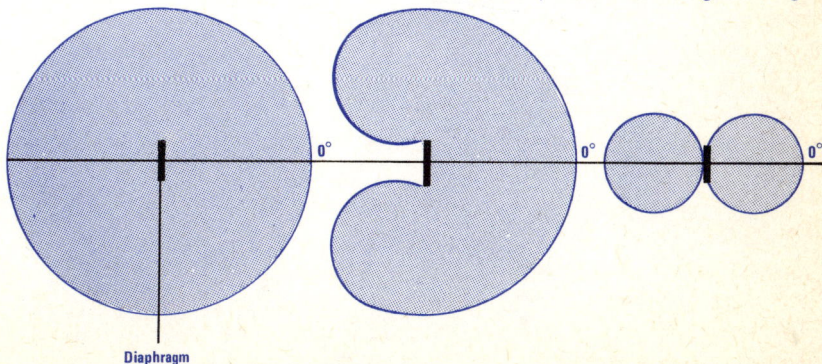

Diaphragm

response lobes produced. Additionally, regardless of type, microphones tend to be directional at high frequencies and omnidirectional at low frequencies.

A crystal microphone will invariably have an omnidirectional polar diagram; a moving coil microphone (incidentally, also referred to as *dynamic*) is nominally omnidirectional, but this response can be modified by acoustic labyrinths within the casing which allow a proportion of the sound energy to reach the back of the diaphragm.

All ribbon microphones have a figure-of-eight polar diagram, the reason for which is obvious if we remember that it operates on the pressure difference principle. Sound waves arriving from the sides, i.e. 90° and 270°, do not cause a pressure difference under ideal conditions, consequently the ribbon does not move. In a normal room, because of random reflections, it will be found that the microphone is not completely dead at the sides but the output is very much reduced. With some ribbon microphones kits of pads are supplied which can be inserted in one side of the casing to modify the response pattern.

Capacitor microphones can be made to any polar diagram and some of the most expensive professional models have a switch box, enabling the response to be changed at will. Because the capacitor microphone has a polarising voltage it is possible to change its characteristics by varying the voltage on the capacitor element. With the other types the differing polar diagrams are obtained by combining pressure operated (omnidirectional) and pressure gradient (figure-of-eight) principles. This can either be

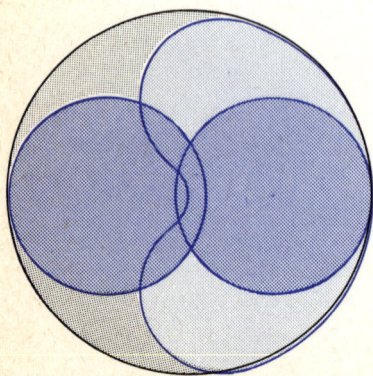

The cardioid response is produced by combining 'pressure gradient' and 'pressure operated' principles.

done by mounting ribbon and moving coil elements in the same casing and combining their outputs electrically; or the physical properties of the case and element can be so designed as to produce the same effect.

Basic Applications

The use of microphones is a very contentious topic and every experienced recording enthusiast has his own views on how they should be placed and which types are most suitable for a particular purpose. As microphone and mixing techniques are discussed in some detail in later chapters, we can confine ourselves here to some general points about the various types.

Crystal microphones are low quality devices; they are robust and cheap, they have a high output voltage and an omnidirectional response. They are not suitable for music recording unless one is desperate: necessity has its own rules! A crystal microphone may be used indoors or out but, as with any microphone used outside, a windshield is essential.

Ribbon microphones are capable of very high quality but they are expensive and fragile and should be treated with respect. They have a low output, a figure-of-eight polar diagram and, in the author's opinion, they are ideal for recording stringed instruments and for speech recording under good acoustic conditions. The ribbon should not be used for the close miking of instruments nor should it be used outdoors. Even quite minor air movements will buffet the ribbon diaphragm and distort the recording, and anything above a gentle breeze is likely to damage the diaphragm irreparably.

Moving coil microphones cover a very wide price range but reasonable musical quality can be obtained for a modest outlay. They are robust and have a fairly high output level and can usually be fed directly into a tape recorder microphone amplifier. They are available with omnidirectional or cardioid responses; under most conditions which the amateur will encounter, the cardioid version will prove superior. They are good general purpose instruments, although lacking the 'truth' of the condenser microphone or the distinctive mellow 'bite' of the ribbon on a string section. A moving coil microphone can be used in or outdoors.

Capacitor microphones are very expensive pieces of equipment but are capable of superb quality from all sound sources. They are reasonably robust but should be protected from damp and, except for the very dearest models, they have either an omnidirectional or a cardioid polar diagram. Again the amateur will find the cardioid more useful. Capacitor microphones have a high output and can be used indoors or out. They are particularly suitable for brass and percussion instruments because of their extended high frequency response.

The properties of microphones which have been discussed in this chapter are summarised in the accompanying table. It is virtually impossible to choose one which will be ideal under all conditions and the novice is probably best advised to begin by buying a moving coil microphone. If he is lucky enough to have friends who are fellow enthusiasts, they could perhaps pool resources and buy a communal capacitor microphone and supplement it with moving coil or ribbon devices, depending on the type of material they intend to record.

Windshield

Before leaping off on your first outdoor recording, do remember that the mesh which covers the front of the microphone casing is not a windshield. A good windshield is an expensive item because it must be acoustically transparent yet prevent interference from wind noise. It usually consists of either a type of plastics foam or a wire grill lined with acoustic material (see page 44). A windshield is effective under reasonable weather conditions, but if the wind is strong it will not be totally so. Indoors a windshield is often useful when working with the type of vocalist who endeavours to sing with the microphone inside his mouth. Not only does it make the microphone more hygienic for subsequent performers, but also it helps protect it from damage and it reduces 'popping' on plosive consonants.

Should a microphone develop a fault it should not be dismantled. However, as few of us seem able to follow such advice, the following words of caution may not come amiss. Do not perform the operation in your workshop, as the powerful magnet in moving coil and ribbon microphones will attract any metal particles in the vicinity. Even non-magnetic dust in the atmosphere will probably cause more problems than the original fault and increase the final repair bill. Treat a microphone with

TABLE

Type	Cost	Polar diagram	Operating principle	Quality	Suggested application	Comments
Crystal	Low	Omnidirectional	Pressure operated; piezo-electric element	Low	Nil	Robust; can be used outdoors; high impedance
Ribbon	Medium/high	Figure-of-eight	Pressure gradient; ribbon diaphragm; moves in magnetic field	Excellent; price a good guide	Speech; music, especially woodwind and strings	Fragile; do not use outdoors; low impedance
Moving coil	Medium/high	Omnidirectional or cardioid	Pressure operated; coil moves in magnetic field	Can be very good	Speech; music, especially brass, bass drum, double bass, percussion	Robust; can be used outdoors; impedance, low, medium or high
Capacitor	Very high	Omnidirectional, cardioid or figure-of-eight; can be switchable	Pressure operated; diaphragm movement varies capacitance; polarising voltage required	Excellent	Speech; music, especially brass and percussion	Fairly robust; can be used outdoors; low impedance is standard

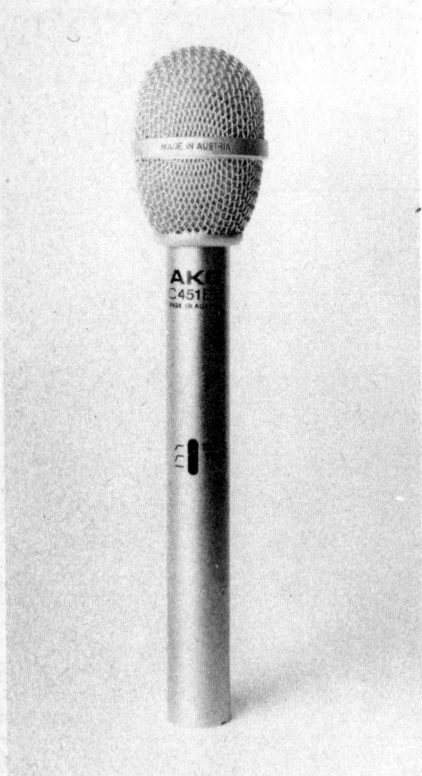

A windshield is an acoustically transparent mesh which protects the diaphragm from buffeting. (Courtesy A.K.G.)

the care you would a microscope and endeavour to carry out repair work under near clinical conditions.

Finally, a word about impedance. The specification both of the microphone and of the tape recorder will quote an impedance figure, either in ohms or, in some cases, simply as high, medium or low. A figure of between 200 and 1000 Ω can be regarded as low; over 1000 and up to 10 000 Ω as medium and over 10 000 Ω as high. For practical purposes it is sufficient that the impedance of the microphone and of the input to which it is connected are of a similar order. A mis-match from low impedance to high will often give acceptable quality. A mis-match from high to low will result in distortion and a very 'thin', or bass light, sound. In general long leads may be used with low impedance devices and not with high. For the serious recordist a low impedance microphone is a better buy, even if it temporarily has to be used with a transformer to match it to the recorder. If in doubt, consult the recorder manufacturer, as he will usually be better informed about impedance matching than your local hi-fi dealer!

4. Mixers, monitoring and installation

We have not so far concerned ourselves with the operational use of the equipment discussed, but rather with the way it works and the facilities required for creative activities. By now the reader will have some general idea of the sort of tape recorder and microphone(s) he requires, and we can move on to the final hardware stage and also consider how everything is connected in a practical set-up.

It will be apparent that any recording which requires more than two microphones, or other sources such as record decks or tape replay machines, will demand more inputs than are available on the recorder. Equally, it is clear that the various sources can more easily be controlled if they are fed to a centralised unit which precedes the recorder. The unit which is used to control and combine the signals is called a *mixer*, and is available in varying degrees of complexity (see page 46).

A number of sources are plugged into the mixer and there is a single output which feeds the recording machine. In order to simplify future descriptions it is necessary to introduce a few terms which will be used when referring to the equipment. The most common sources are record players, tape decks and microphones—these are known respectively as *gram, tape* and *mic*. The sources are plugged to *inputs* and each input is associated with a *channel*. In order to control the level of an individual input, each channel has a volume control, known as a

45

fader. The *record machine* is also known as the *assembly machine* and to differentiate between this and a replay machine, it is common to refer to tape sources as *inserts*. The set-up from source through to record machine and monitor is known as a *signal chain*, and the links in this chain can now be discussed in more detail.

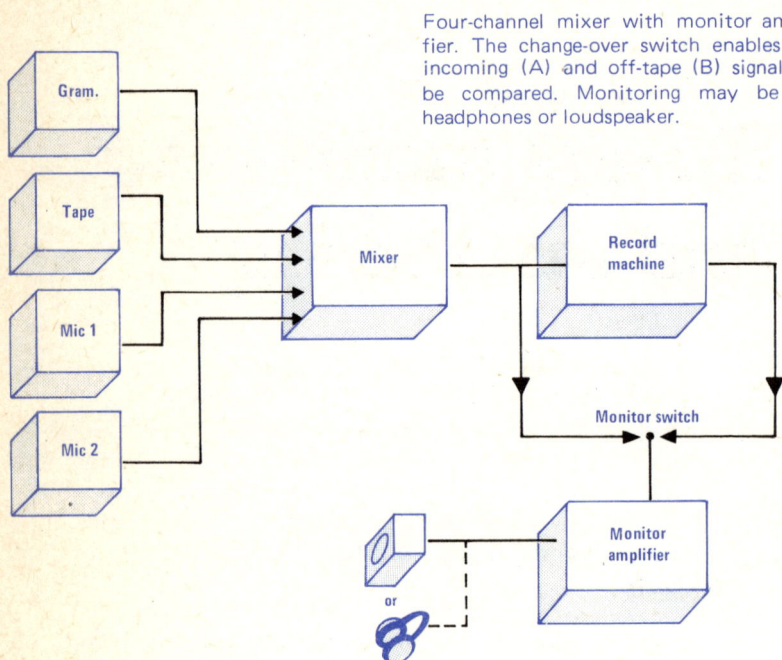

Four-channel mixer with monitor amplifier. The change-over switch enables the incoming (A) and off-tape (B) signals to be compared. Monitoring may be by headphones or loudspeaker.

Basic Equipment

For economic reasons the tape replay (insert) machine will probably be rather less sophisticated than the record machine described in Chapter 2. The plan here is to work as part of a creative team and persuade a friend to provide a good quality insert machine. A gram unit is required not only for playing material directly into the 'production' but also for dubbing insert material on to tape. This will be dealt with in detail later, but there are many instances in which it is more convenient to use a tape than a gram source.

The gram deck should preferably be of transcription quality and have a 12 in (30 cm) turntable; ideally it should be manually operated, have an easily adjustable pickup arm and a good

Simplified block diagram of a basic stereo
mixer. Each input can be switched to either
the left- or right-hand group.

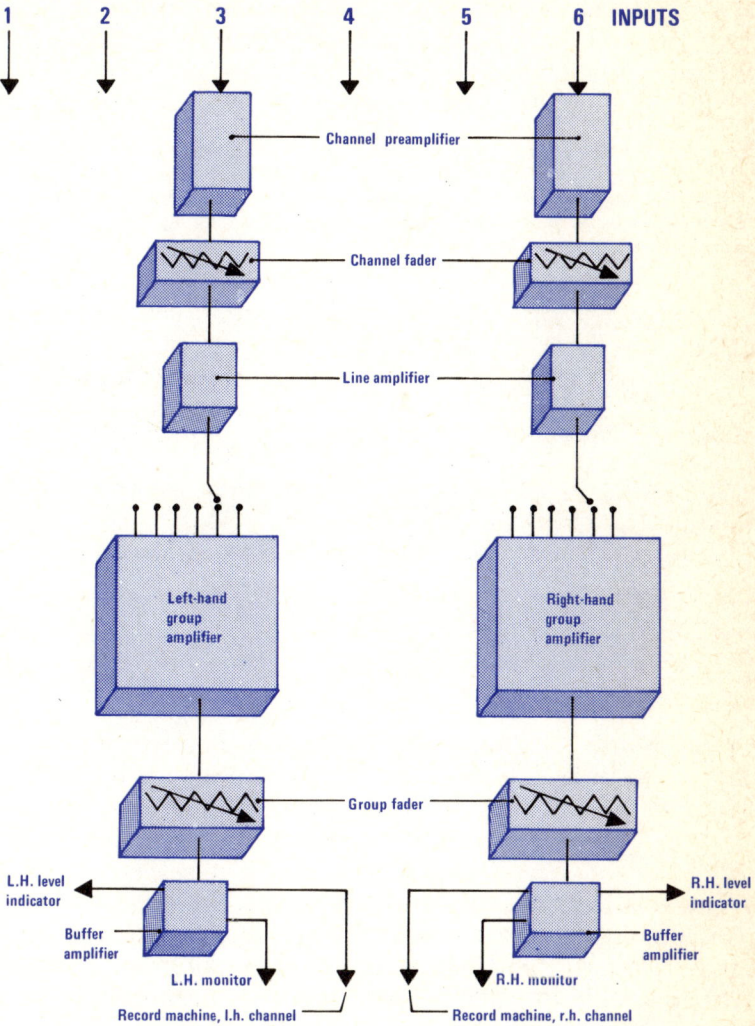

1 2 3 4 5 6 **INPUTS**

Channel preamplifier

Channel fader

Line amplifier

Left-hand
group
amplifier

Right-hand
group
amplifier

Group fader

L.H. level
indicator

R.H. level
indicator

Buffer
amplifier

Buffer
amplifier

L.H. monitor

R.H. monitor

Record machine, l.h. channel

Record machine, r.h. channel

magnetic cartridge. For operational work, especially where quick
cueing is concerned, the arm should be set so that the cartridge is
working at the top end of its tracking weight range. Depending
on the type of turntable, it may be found convenient to fit a toggle
switch on the plinth to interrupt the supply voltage to the motor.   47

(If the drive system is engaged with the toggle switch off, a rapid start can be obtained on many turntables by operating the toggle switch.) This is worth experimenting with, but if the turntable has an idler wheel drive be sure not to leave it engaged for too long with the turntable stationary. The resultant pressure causes 'flats' on the idler which produce wow. Another useful modification to the turntable, to give an instant start, is an aluminium disc 13 or 14 in (33 or 36 cm) in diameter with a centre hole which fits the

For creative work an instant start of the turntable is often required. In some cases this can be obtained by wiring a toggle switch in series with the mains on/off switch (A). Another method is to fit an aluminium disc of larger diameter than the turntable. The disc can be held with the turntable running and when released it will rapidly run up to speed (B).

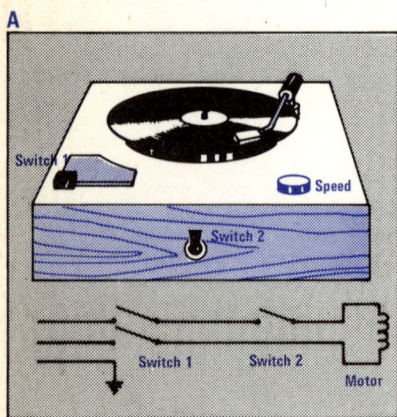

turntable spindle. If this is placed on top of the turntable mat, the edge of the plate can be held whilst the turntable is revolving: when the plate is released an almost instant start will be obtained. Both the above ideas require a reasonably powerful drive motor.

We have already discussed microphones and there is nothing we need to add about mic sources at this stage, except that it is, of course, essential to confirm that they are compatible in terms of sensitivity and impedance (see Chapter 3) with the mixer inputs.

Mixer

As far as the mixer itself is concerned, it must be both electronically and operationally suitable for creative work.

On the electronic side, the minimum number of channels required is four but six give very much more flexibility, and even larger numbers will be required for recording pop music. The specified performance of the mixer should be better than that of the recorder; ideally it should be as good as a high quality preamplifier and in no circumstances should it be electronically inferior to the recording machine, otherwise the sound quality will suffer.

The important parameters are S/N ratio, frequency response and distortion. In Chapter 2 we gave some typical figures for the performance of a good quality tape recorder. With a mixer we would expect on the mic and gram inputs an unweighted S/N ratio in the order of 70dB, with reference to the mixer's maximum output level, and on high level inputs a ratio of 80dB. With all channels fully open the S/N ratio should not deteriorate to less than 60dB. All input stages should have an overload margin of at least 40dB (voltage ratio of 100:1) above the nominal input sensitivity before the onset of audible distortion. In the case of a mic input having a sensitivity of 0.1mV, this means that overload should not occur until the signal exceeds 10mV. This S/N specification is quite modest by professional standards but reasonably demanding in terms of domestic sound mixing equipment. Obviously one should regard the mixer and record machine as complementary units and try to allocate the available cash so that they are both of a similar standard.

The frequency response should be virtually flat from 30Hz to 20kHz and ideally each channel should have a switched bass and treble filter. Distortion should be below 0.1% from the input of any channel to the mixer output. Detailed specifications of mixer units can be found in the *Hi-Fi Year Book*, published annually in October by IPC Electrical-Electronic Press Ltd., London, and by writing to the manufacturers of portable equipment. The handyman can make considerable savings by building a mixer from one of the proprietary kit specialists. Alternatively, the practical hi-fi and electronics magazines often carry constructional articles on making equipment of this type.

The sensitivity of several of the channel inputs is frequently switchable so that they will accept either high or low level signals—say tape or mic. Naturally this facility adds to the price but the expense is justified by the gain in flexibility. Unless a mixer channel has a specific *equalised* gram input it will not be possible to plug the output of a pickup direct to a channel. This is because the output from a cartridge is not flat and the response has to be modified (or equalised) before the signal can be fed to the channel amplifier. If none of the mixer inputs is equalised, a suitable preamplifier can be obtained from certain cartridge manufacturers or ordered through an audio retailer. The preamplifier is small enough to be fitted inside most turntable plinths, and the output is then fed to a high level mixer channel.

In many recording situations it is important to be able to listen to a particular source before it is faded up on the mixer. This facility is known as *pre-hear* or *pre-fade* and is only likely to be found on more expensive equipment. A competent audio engineer should be able to modify an existing mixer at relatively low cost.

In order to control levels accurately and to feed a well balanced signal to the record machine, it is necessary to be able to monitor the output from the mixer. Ideally the mixer should have a meter or other visual indication of sound level, as well as a headphone or loudspeaker output for the checking of sound balance and quality. Headphones will be necessary if the mics and the mixer are in the same room, as the use of a loudspeaker will cause acoustic feedback.

Operational Convenience

For convenience and to avoid physical discomfort, which affects concentration, the mixer should be installed so that it can be

It is often necessary to listen to a source before it is faded up on the mixer. The block diagram shows how a mixer can be modified to give this facility. It is advisable to consult a competent audio engineer before attempting such a modification.

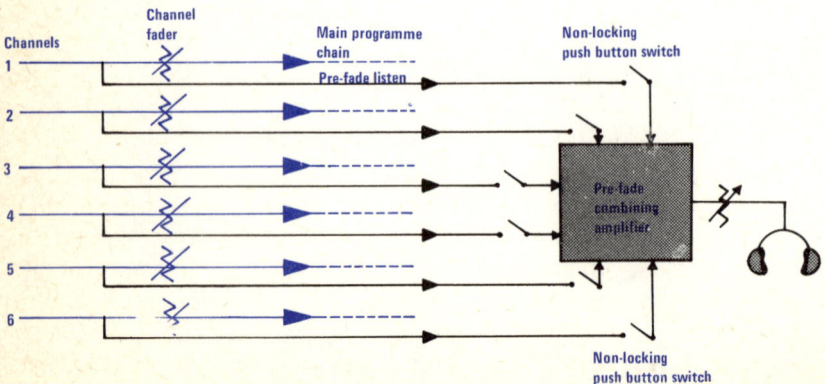

operated from a seated position. From an engineering point of view it is immaterial whether the sliding type of fader is fitted or the more traditional rotary control, but operationally it is important (see pages 52 and 53). The human hand is capable of turning one knob at a time, though some gifted mortals manage to rotate a pair of adjacent knobs single-handed with a fair degree of precision. With linear motion faders, it is possible for each hand to control up to five faders with a reasonable degree of accuracy. Obviously in a situation such as sound mixing, where a number of controls must be operated either simultaneously or in quick succession, the sliding control has many advantages. It is also important that there is sufficient space between all regularly used controls for one to be operated without the fingers disturbing the setting of another. At the same time the controls should be logically arranged and come easily to hand, with the most frequently required ones being most readily accessible.

If the mixer is standing on a box or table, even if the height is well chosen, it will frequently be found that the wrist position is unnatural when the faders are being used. This can only be determined by giving the device a thorough workout before purchasing it. Choosing a mixer is rather like choosing a car: it is irrelevant what colour it is or what shape if it is a misery to drive. Generally a mixer is easier to operate if the controls are on a horizontal rather than a vertical panel. Also take note where the input and output sockets are situated, as many designers are notoriously impractical. A mixer is useless if it has sockets located near operational controls such as faders, because when the various leads are plugged in they will obstruct one's access to, and control of, the knobs. It is far better if the connections are made via a rear or side panel, as this not only leaves the front panel clear but also lessens the chances of tripping over the cables. The resultant loss of dignity is not too important, but if the mixer rapidly follows you to the floor it could seriously affect your marital prospects!

The points mentioned are the most important considerations when selecting a mixing unit. Naturally the final choice will depend on the envisaged application and on the cost, appearance, personal design preferences and other common sense factors which need not be laboured here. But remember, it is a creative tool you are acquiring: it must feel right, it must be logically arranged and it must be flexible.

51

Linear sliding faders are operationally
more satisfactory than rotary ones, and a
horizontal (or slightly inclined) panel is
less fatiguing to use than a vertical one.
In the illustrations A is a better design
than B. Cables should be connected to the
side or rear panels of the mixer.

A

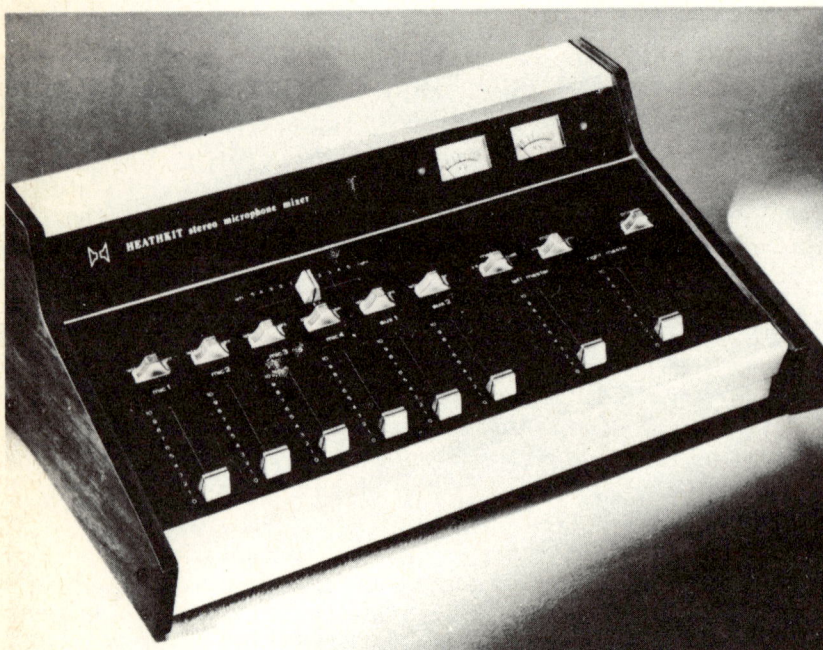

Connections

Many enthusiasts feel that selecting the right equipment is the
hardest task the recordist has to perform; others have a distinct
attack of nausea when faced with lengths of anonymous
connecting cable. In fact there is no great mystery about wiring up
audio systems and anyone who is not at home with a soldering
iron can purchase cables ready-fitted with the required plugs.

Earthing

If the reader heeds only one piece of advice in this book, then make
it this one: before switching on any equipment ensure that the
mains plug is correctly wired and that all accessible metalwork is

B

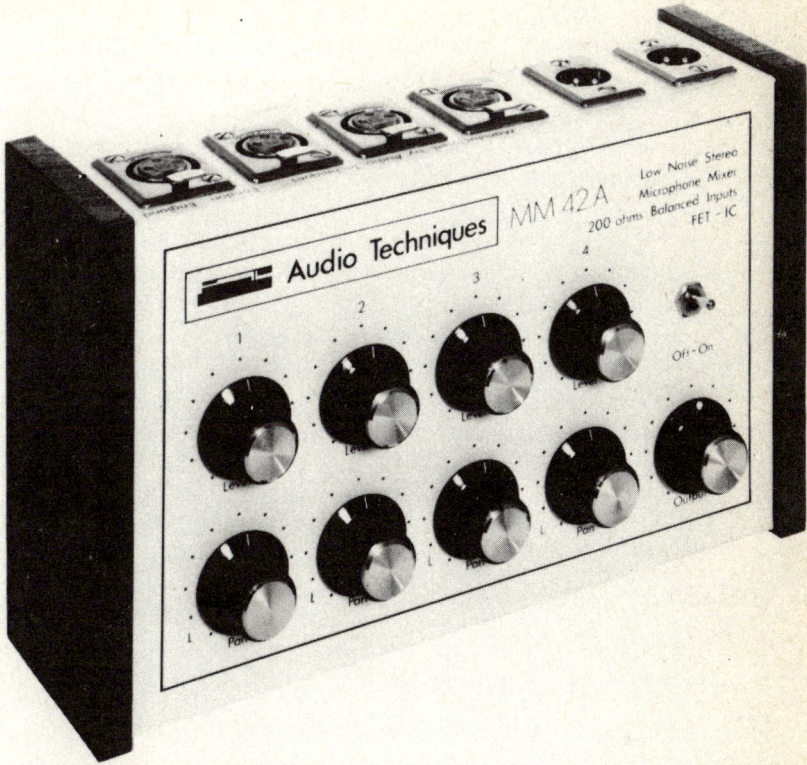

There must be only one earth point.
Multiple earthing causes earth currents in
the signal leads which result in hum.

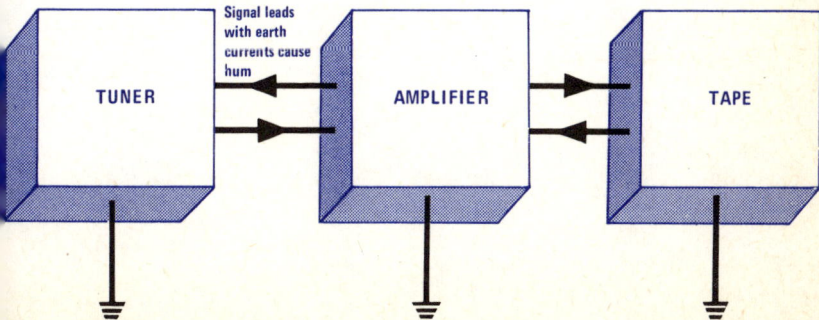

properly earthed*. Most of the problems which arise in wiring domestic audio systems result from poor or incorrect earthing or from a multiplicity of earth points. It is essential that there is only one path to earth for the entire installation, because if several points are earthed separately an *earth loop* will be formed and may cause hum (page 53). This is due to minute currents at mains frequency affecting input cables and high sensitivity preamplifiers. The correct wiring approach is to earth a selected piece of equipment and to earth everything else back to this point.

In practice it may not be that straightforward and a certain amount of trial and error may be necessary to eliminate earth loops. Frequently it will be found that mains operated equipment is fitted with a two-core supply cable. Sometimes a separate earth terminal will be provided on the chassis but in many cases earthing is totally ignored. In other instances the woven wire screen around the audio leads, which acts as the signal return, is also used for earthing. But again there are examples where the signal return is not connected to any external metal work.

If the amplifier is earthed, the other equipment should not be earthed at the junction box but via the amplifier. The earth path in some cases is completed by the screening braid of the audio cables.

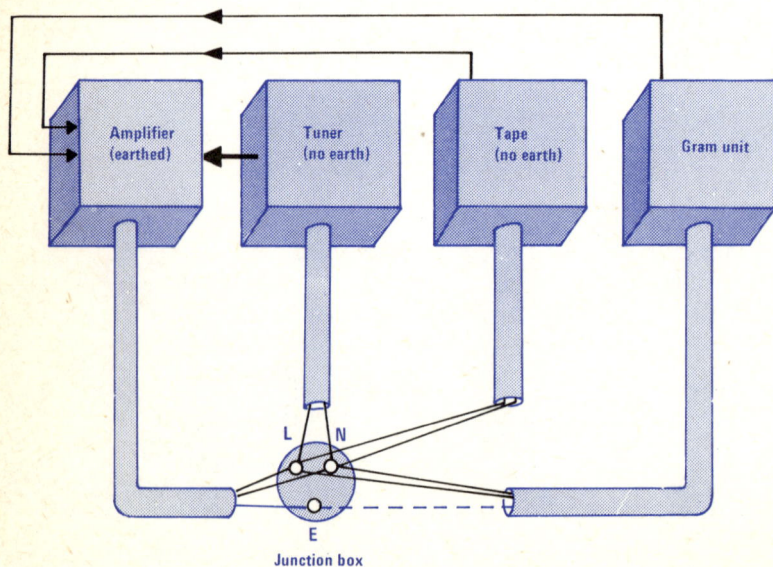

Amplifier (earthed)

Tuner (no earth)

Tape (no earth)

Gram unit

L N

E

Junction box

*Or grounded

The correct wiring approach depends on whether an installation is a permanent fixture in, say, a spare room which is to be used as a 'studio'; or whether it has to be readily transportable for assembly in a location such as a village hall. In the first case the mains connections can be made to a ringmain junction box and a single lead taken out to a wall point. In the second case it is probably worth making wooden trolleys to support the equipment and to plug the various units to a mains extension block with multiple outlets.

Whether the set-up is permanent or portable, all equipment which has a three-core mains lead should have all three wires connected, initially, following the standard colour code. Equipment having only two-core cable frequently conforms to no known colour coding standard: the two wires may even have identical sleeving! If blue and black leads are used, which is often the case with units of European origin, black is usually 'line' and blue 'neutral' but there are exceptions to this. Where possible, two-core leads should be connected to three-pin or other non-reversible plugs, because sometimes mains hum can be reduced by reversing the polarity of the supply to a particular piece of equipment. Once the most favourable wiring combination has been found the non-reversible plug will prevent future uncertainty.

Safety

With regard to polarity, certain precautions should be taken when connecting a.c./d.c. equipment as it is possible for the chassis to be 'live'. This is not a hazard under normal conditions when the equipment is operated alone: in fact many televisions are in daily use with a 'live' chassis. The problem only arises when a fault occurs or if another piece of equipment is plugged to that with the 'live' chassis. For this reason if you wish to record from your television, take expert advice before connecting any external apparatus. A neon screwdriver is invaluable for checking the polarity of equipment which is being interconnected. If the neon glows when the screwdriver is touched against the chassis or any exposed metalwork, the mains wiring should be checked immediately and no interconnection made to any equipment with a 'live' chassis.

Eliminating Hum

Having made the mains connections, the audio leads are plugged one by one and each input checked for hum before the next is plugged. If hum is present, try removing the earth connection from the offending unit: the hum may disappear or change in character, or there may be no significant difference. If the hum disappears it is possible simply to cut off the 'offending' earth. Before doing this, check that there is an alternative earth path. This may be provided by the screen of the audio cable or by a flying lead connecting, say, the turntable to the amplifier. A typical example is illustrated. The pickup harness incorporates a lead with a tag at either end. One tag is connected to a terminal on the amplifier and the other to the metalwork of the gram deck. If this is done the mains earth on the three-core cable from the gram motor is not required—*provided the amplifier is earthed.* It is not

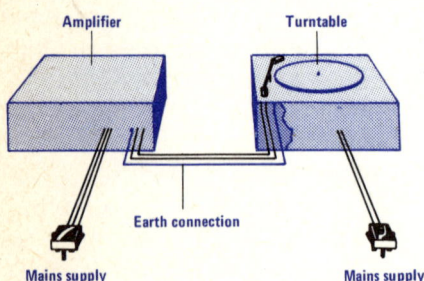

Amplifier

Turntable

Earth connection

Mains supply

Mains supply

When connecting a gram unit, a flying lead is often used to provide a mains earth from the amplifier to the deck plate of the gram.

possible to cover the many variations which will be encountered in practice and even if what appears to be a logical approach is adopted, some experimentation may be necessary.

If a simple test meter is available with a resistance scale for testing continuity, then it is very easy to check that all exposed metalwork is earthed. If a meter is not available a bell battery, bulb and a pair of flying leads can be used instead.

Once the set-up is working satisfactorily it is well worthwhile identifying the various cables. Then if the equipment is re-plugged or the installation is changed or moved, everything can be reconnected with a minimum of difficulty. There are several simple ways of identifying cables, the cheapest of which is to use self-adhesive paper strips marked with a suitable abbreviation or symbol. The strip is wrapped around the barrel of the plug, or the cable itself, and then covered with clear cellulose tape for protection. Other forms of identification are numbered cable rings which are available from electrical wholesalers, or coloured rubber sleeves. Equipment panels can be marked with Letraset or Dymo marking tape.

After installing the equipment check that all exposed metal work is earthed. Use either a test meter or a battery and bulb with flying leads.

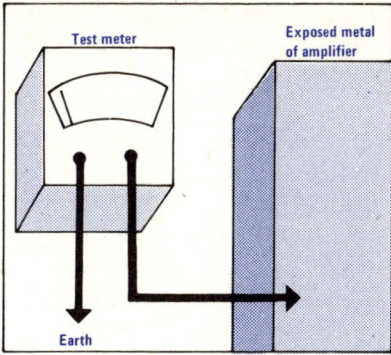

Test meter · Exposed metal of amplifier · Earth

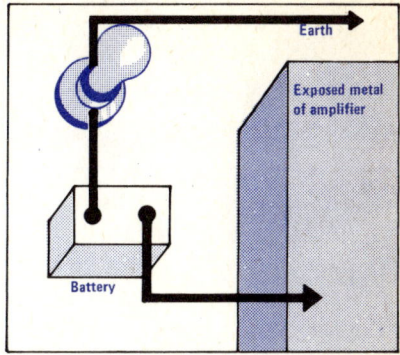

Earth · Exposed metal of amplifier · Battery

Organisation

The way in which the equipment is laid out will depend on the particular application. Obviously there are no hard and fast rules and everyone develops his own way of working, but two essentials are comfort and space to read a script with ease. It is advantageous to use a two-man team for recording, with one man acting as sound mixer whilst the other controls the record machine and operates the tape and gram decks. If the tape and gram work is too involved for one man either another can be drafted into the team or the sound mixer can play some of the tape inserts. These

It is convenient to have two operators on many recording sessions. ·One man operates the mixer and possibly the record machine; the other operates the gram unit(s) and tape insert machines.

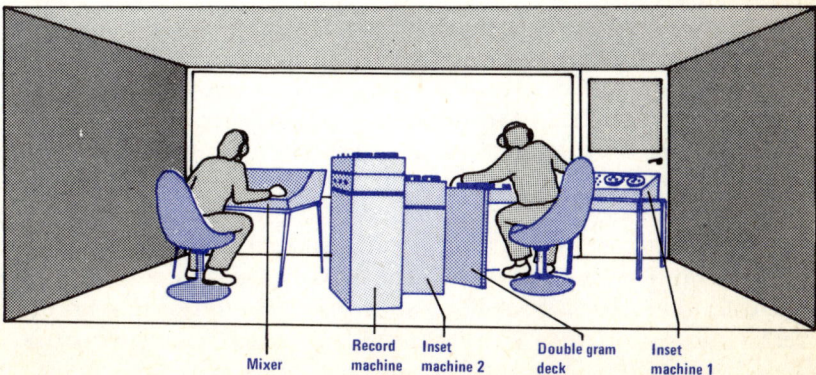

Mixer · Record machine · Inset machine 2 · Double gram deck · Inset machine 1

comments apply more, of course, to drama and feature recording than to music. The set-up illustrated is fairly elaborate, such as might be used in a village hall in collaboration with a local drama group, but it can be simplified to suit circumstances.

Monitoring

Earlier it was mentioned that if the mixing equipment is in the same room as the microphones, monitoring will have to be done using headphones. Wherever possible an attempt should be made to devise a recording set-up where monitoring is possible by loudspeaker. However, if loudspeaker monitoring can only be done at low level, it will be preferable to wear headphones, as it is not possible properly to balance and control a recording if the listening level is too low.

The problem is that the ear is more sensitive at mid frequencies than it is at the extremes of the audio range. As the sound level is progressively reduced the subjective effect is that there is a loss of bass and treble. For this reason it is important to monitor at a fairly high level, though there is no need to carry one's enthusiasm to ridiculous lengths! The listening level should be well below the threshold of pain or one's hearing may be damaged. This is a particular danger when recording pop music, especially if electronic instruments are used. In this respect some types of headphone represent a greater danger than loudspeakers, as the ear is totally enclosed and subjected to high sound intensities.

Listening Levels

When he has gained a certain amount of experience, the recordist will find that he has a preferred listening level: a level to which he returns automatically and at which he feels comfortable. He should try always to work within this comfort region and resist being tempted to stray too far from it. Whereas the monitoring level can be set to suit the individual, the recording level is governed partially by technical limitations. In order to work within the given limits a level meter is required, which may be on the record machine or incorporated in the mixer. If it is on the record machine, this must be positioned so that it is easily visible from the mixing desk. If it is on the mixer a suitable setting of the record level control should be determined by experiment and the knob removed or its position marked. Thereafter level control is carried out at the mixing desk.

Dynamic Range

To make a technically satisfactory recording a number of conflicting requirements have to be met. If the signal level is too low when recording, the system noise (i.e. tape hiss plus amplifier noise) will be obtrusive on replay and mar the sound quality. If the signal level is too high this will result in severe distortion at mid to low frequencies and tape saturation at high frequencies. The dynamic range of the recording must therefore be kept within the upper and lower limits, and the object of level control is to achieve the optimum dynamic range whilst ensuring that the tape is neither too quiet nor over-modulated. The dynamic range of music (i.e. that between the quietest and the loudest sounds) greatly exceeds that which can be recorded and the art of sound mixing is to work within the technical limitations without audibly degrading the quality or balance of the recording. We will expand upon this when specific recording situations are discussed in later chapters.

5. Improvising a studio

For the most part domestic recordings will probably have to be made in a normal room which is temporarily converted into a studio. The big problem always is to find somewhere which is acoustically satisfactory, a problem best illustrated if you go around the house from room to room and clap loudly—once—in the centre of each room. You will notice that a clap in the bathroom has a brittle reverberant character; in the hall it is sharp but less reverberant and in the living room the clap is much more quickly absorbed but will often excite a 'ring' or resonance from ornaments within the room.

Reverberation Time

In each room the clap will take a finite but different time to die away. The decay at a given frequency for a particular room is constant unless the room is physically changed in some way. This decay is known as the *reverberation time* and is defined as the time taken for a sound of constant intensity to fall in level by 60 dB after the original sound has stopped, 60 dB being a ratio of 1 000 000:1.

Standing Waves

The floor covering, wall decoration, type of curtaining, bookcases and the amount of soft furnishing will determine the time a sound takes to decay. However, a room may have a satisfactory reverberation time but be unsuitable for recording because of multiple reflections, particularly from opposite walls. Any room which has hard parallel surfaces will produce standing waves (or *eigentones*). For every room dimension there is a corresponding sound wavelength. When a note is sounded which

Reverberation time is the time taken for the steady state sound level in a room to fall in intensity by 60 dB.

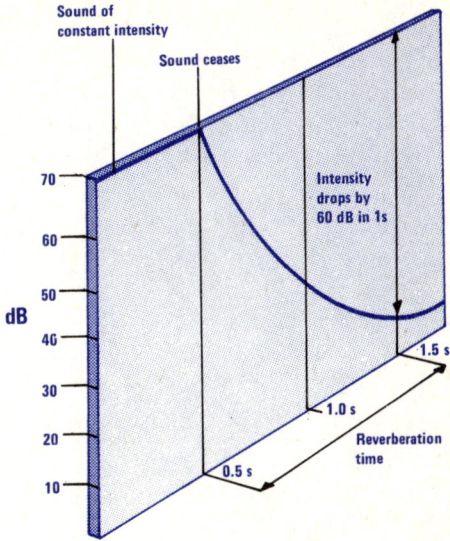

has a comparable wavelength an eigentone is set up as the sound wave bounces to and fro between parallel surfaces like a high velocity ping-pong ball. The eigentones occur at multiples of half a wavelength and a rectangular room will therefore have a harmonic series of eigentones in proportion to the height, length and width of the room.

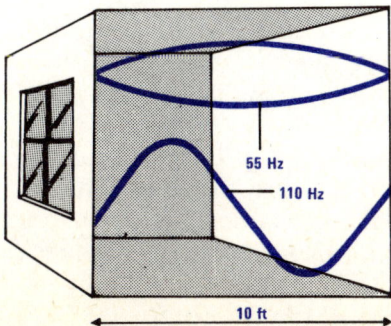

Standing waves. The room has walls 10 ft (3 m) apart. The speed of sound is 1100 ft/s (330 m/s). A sound having a wavelength of 10 ft (3 m) has a frequency of 110 Hz. The first standing wave occurs when distance between walls = ½ wavelength: therefore for 10 ft (3 m) spacing the fundamental standing wave is at 55 Hz.

61

The effect of eigentones is to cause coloration of the recorded sound: this gives a characteristic boominess to small rooms which performers can find very distracting. As an example, a room measuring 10 x 8 x 12 ft (3.0 x 2.4 x 3.7 m) will have fundamental resonances at 55, 68 and 46 Hz respectively. An improvement can be obtained if the walls are covered with materials of varying thickness. Curtains or eiderdowns can be draped in folds to cover some of the larger expanses of wall. Bookcases, particularly if they are full of irregularly shaped books, will help to disperse the reflections.

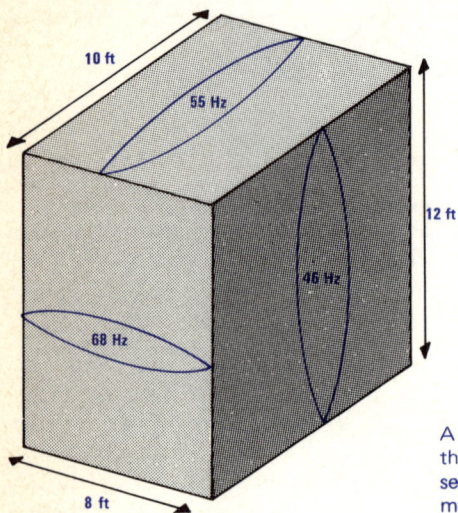

A rectangular room has standing waves in three planes and there is a harmonic sequence of such waves. Only the fundamental is shown.

Extraneous Noise

We can see, then, that a room's suitability for recording depends mainly on its shape, size and furnishing, but another major consideration is the degree to which the room is isolated from extraneous sounds. It is important to remember that a microphone is not selective in the way that the ear is. In a crowded room, or at a concert, we can direct our attention to a particular area and discriminate against unwanted sound. The microphone cannot do this: if it is omnidirectional it will pick up sound from all angles, but even if it is nominally directional it will still respond to reflections and to all sounds, wanted and unwanted, arriving 'on axis'. Nothing can be done at a later stage to eliminate this unwanted noise. An obvious example is that of a recording made of a meeting in a room near a main road. The ear will quickly adapt and learn to reject the traffic noise and concentrate on the voice it wishes to hear. The microphone will give equal importance to all sounds and it will faithfully scramble together the various conversations and the external traffic noise. This will be all too apparent when the tape is played back.

If you live in a noisy location there is little you can do but try to use a room away from the road and endeavour to record at a time of day that experience has shown to be fairly quiet. If you are fortunate enough to have a choice of rooms, look for one with plenty of soft furnishings as mentioned earlier, but also test the floor boards for creaks and check that the door is substantial enough to give a degree of isolation from the domestic sounds in the rest of the house. It is a good idea to make a series of test recordings in the possible rooms to find which one gives the best initial results and then try to improve that room. It is amazingly difficult to *ad lib* intelligently into a microphone and probably the best plan is to read a few paragraphs from a book or newspaper in each room. If extraneous noise can get in, it is clear that noise from your 'studio' can get out and it is advisable to have a certain amount of consideration for neighbours! The best approach, of course, is to try to involve them in your project.

Sound Proofing

Even amongst experienced technicians there tends to be some confused thinking about acoustic treatment and sound proofing. Sound proofing requires weight, physical separation and an insulating medium between the inside and outside, the object being to cause the sound wave to expend its energy in trying to penetrate the wall and the insulating medium. The more changes of medium the sound wave has to negotiate to escape the better, e.g. air-to-brick-to-air-to-brick-to-air as in a cavity wall. Each change of medium will attenuate the sound further and the resultant leakage will be very low. Similarly double glazing is very effective, but for sound insulation the air gap between panes should be at least 4 in (102 mm). Domestic double glazing for reducing heat loss will give a measure of sound proofing but it will be less effective than if a wider spacing were used. There is very little that can be done in the average home to reduce sound transmission from room to room or through a single party wall, unless quite major structural alteration is undertaken.

No amount of acoustic treatment within a room (i.e. egg boxes on the wall and polystyrene tiles all over the place) will significantly affect the level of noise escaping from or entering the recording room. The purpose of acoustic treatment is to reduce reflections within the room and to ensure that such reflections as do exist are dispersed to avoid unpleasant room resonances. These internal reflections are treated by various types of absorber which act in a similar way to fishing nets: sound is allowed to pass through but not to return. If the difference between a sound absorber and sound proofing is not clear, imagine an open window. This is the ultimate absorber and sound is neither reflected into the room nor impeded from leaving it. We therefore have maximum absorption and minimum sound proofing.

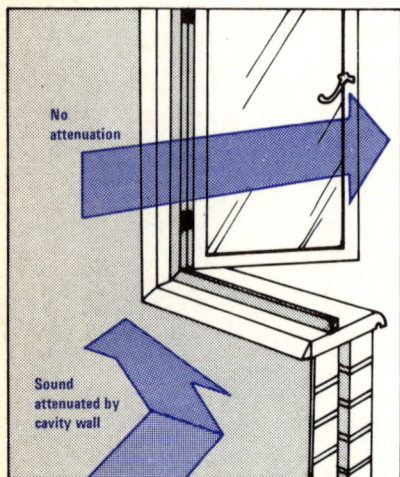

Absorption and reflection. The open window allows all sound to escape; thus it is effectively an infinite absorber. It gives no sound proofing. The cavity wall reflects sound into the room and thus gives little absorption. It allows little sound to pass through and so gives good sound insulation.

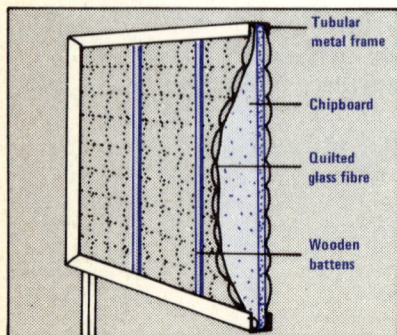

Acoustic screen constructed from a tubular metal frame with a chipboard insert. A piece of chipboard is mounted in a free standing frame of square tubing and faced with layers of glass fibre insulation secured by strips of pegboard. Experiments can then be made with various drapes hanging in folds on top of the pegboard.

It is clear then that acoustic tiles and the like give no protection against extraneous noise. What they will do is to modify the reverberation time and acoustic character of the room. As we have seen it will sound echoey if the walls are bare, and parallel surfaces will cause standing waves. Even if it is impracticable to change the furnishing or decoration of the room, considerable benefits can be obtained by improvising portable screens.

If several such frames are made they will prove useful in a variety of situations. For example, a corner of a room can be boxed off to make a booth for a narrator, where a relatively dead acoustic and intimate microphone technique are required. In a hall screens can be used to modify the character of one or two areas to create the effect of different environments. When recording music, they can be used to give separation between instruments by preventing the sound from one instrument from spilling on to the mic of another. The drums are a prime offender here, but it is usual for the front screen to be just low enough to give the drummer visual contact with the other performers. It is very helpful to leave the backs of the screens untreated so that they have an acoustically hard and a soft side; then by simply turning them around the character of the sound can be changed.

In general music requires a relatively long reverberation time and speech recording a relatively short one. Also, speech is restricted to a much narrower band of frequencies and therefore less compromises are called for when recording speech in a domestic

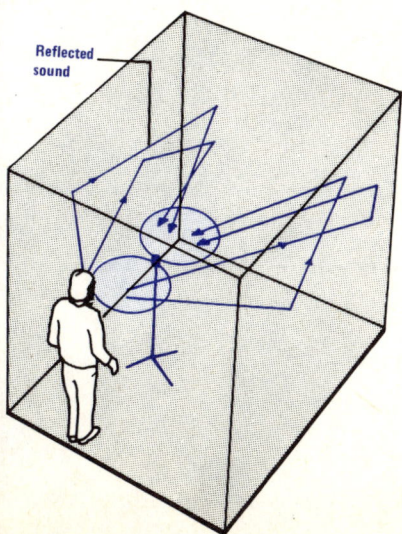

Reflected sound

Direct sound is followed, after a short interval, by reflected indirect sound.

room than when recording music. It is probably better to aim at simple modifications to a room, as outlined earlier, to produce a favourable acoustic for speech recording. Then for music one of the commercially available echo springs or tape delay units can be used to add a measure of artificial reverberation. This will be dealt with in more detail in Chapter 8, where music recording is discussed.

If a speech recording is made in an over-reverberant room, the direct sound wave arriving at the microphone is followed a short time later by a series of waves reflected from various surfaces (see page 65). As a result words and syllables appear to run together and the recording is indistinct. If the room is close carpeted it is doubtful if floor reflections can be significantly reduced, but if there are areas of vinyl tiles or wood block flooring, try rolling out an old piece of carpet. When working in a village hall or away from home it is useful to carry a number of carpet tiles for this purpose, which can easily be laid where required.

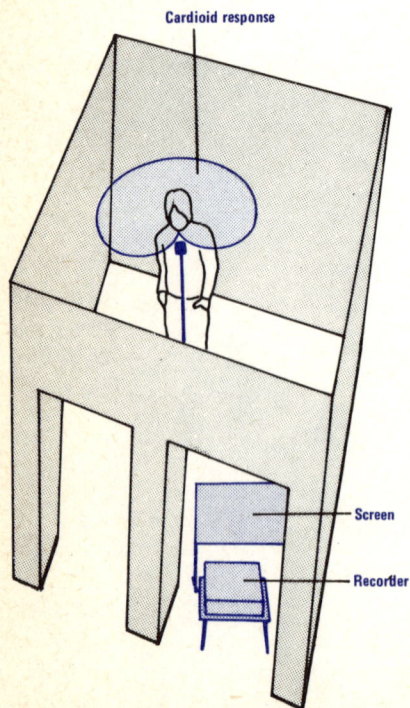

Cardioid response

Position the recorder as far away from the microphone as possible, preferably in an alcove and on the dead side of the mic. An acoustic screen may help.

Screen

Recorder

Monitoring

In Chapter 4 we explained that if the microphones and the recording equipment are in the same room, monitoring has to be done on headphones to prevent acoustic feedback. If you are working in a small room, the problem then arises that any mechanical noise produced by the equipment will be picked up by the microphones. This is very difficult to avoid. An acoustic screen between equipment and microphone may help, and thick foam rubber underneath the recorder will prevent the table from acting as a sounding board. If possible place the recording equipment in an alcove, say alongside a chimney breast, and use directional microphones, positioned so that the equipment is to the dead side of the mic.

When using a hall it may be possible to use an adjacent room as a control booth and monitor on loudspeakers. Much will depend on the sound isolation between the two rooms. Most creative recording work requires a degree of visual contact between the performers and the operational staff. In the ideal case this is obtained by a double-glazed panel between the studio and the control room, but the amateur will rarely be able to work in this way. Probably the best he can hope for is to peer through a projectionist's window or pass signals via an intermediary. If visual communication is not possible, one has to decide whether the isolation of a separate room with its consequent ease of operation is sufficient compensation, or whether communication is essential. In the latter case headphone monitoring is the only answer. It may be that the level of mechanical noise is such that it is impracticable to start and stop insert machines whilst the recording is taking place. The answer then is to record the 'live' speeches under the quietest possible conditions and to edit in any insert material later. These techniques will be discussed in more detail in the appropriate chapter.

Communication

Should you be lucky with your choice of hall it may be possible to make use of existing cable ducts and lay microphone cables in a semi-permanent fashion. Then all one has to do at the beginning of a session is to plug in the mixing and monitoring equipment at one end and the microphones at the other. If the studio and control room are isolated, it is a good idea to install a simple talkback system so that the operational staff can talk to the actors. What is required are a relatively cheap microphone and amplifier which are connected to a small loudspeaker in the studio. The microphone should have an on/off switch, and some trial and error will be necessary to establish a set-up which does not produce feedback. It will probably be necessary to arrange for the microphone switch to operate a relay which mutes the control room loudspeaker whilst the talkback mic is live.

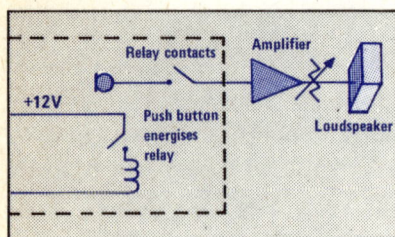

Simple talkback system. The push button energises a relay which connects the microphone to the amplifier.

Studio Furniture

Having satisfied, within practical limits, the acoustic requirements of the studio, it is worth paying some attention to the studio furniture. For most kinds of music recording chairs will be required for the musicians, but when recording drama it is usually better if the actors are standing. They then find it easier to get into character and are also able to vary their working distance from the microphone, for effect, when required. Recorded narration and free discussion are different again and here it is helpful if the performers have chairs and a table, as they are then anchored to a particular position and thus more under the sound balancer's control. The best type of chair to use is the tubular metal type, sometimes known as a stacking chair, and readily available in halls that are regularly used for meetings. Wooden chairs should be avoided where possible because they tend to creak at the most unfortunate moments!

When a table is used, either for discussion purposes or because a narrator has a script to keep in order, it is important again to ensure that it is sufficiently solid not to creak if leaned upon. At the same time it should not have a solid smooth top, otherwise reflections from it will give coloration to, and cause degradation of, the speech quality. It helps if the table top is covered with several layers of blanket and the microphone suspended from an overhead stand rather than resting on the table. If constructing a table for studio use, build a solid frame but make the top on a sort of lattice principle and stretch an open-weave fabric across the lattice to form the table top. This will be solid enough to support a script (and elbows if the struts are not too far apart) but it will be reasonably transparent to speech frequencies and so prevent reflections.

Microphone Stands

Under the heading of furniture should also be included microphone stands, as these are a very necessary accessory to any recording session. Except on the most dire economic grounds, or when recording an interview outdoors, there is no excuse for using a hand held microphone. It is a technique which requires a great deal of practice and most performers if given a hand mic will use it incorrectly, ruining what could otherwise have been a good recording. The main offences are working too close, excessive or unnecessary movement and handling noise due to finger move-

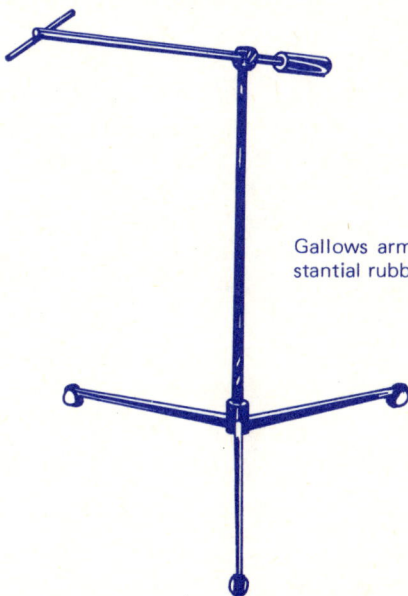

Gallows arm microphone stand with substantial rubber feet.

ment on the barrel of the mic. For most purposes the boom or 'gallows arm' type of stand can be used: it is robust, it can be adjusted to almost any angle and it is fairly well isolated from mechanical shock. When choosing this type of stand try to obtain the type with folding legs, as this makes for easy storage; also check that it is fitted with substantial rubber feet.

There are many inferior versions of this type of stand on the market: make sure that yours has good quality tubing which does not whip, and that it will not overbalance with the boom extended horizontally and a microphone attached. Also check that it can be adjusted easily, but when placed in position that it stays there. If you are seriously bothered by structure-borne noise, some improvement may be obtained by decoupling the microphone from the stand. One way of doing this is to attach some short elastic luggage straps to the stand and to suspend the microphone from these. Sufficient elastic should be used for the microphone not to bob around like a cork, but at the same time it must not be stiff enough to reduce the decoupling effect.

Stands can, of course, be improvised from bamboo poles, or from old pieces of piping with a bolt of the appropriate thread bonded to one end. The pole or pipe is then lashed to a table or chair so that the microphone is at the required angle. This is one step better than holding the mic in a sweaty fist but it is a very impracticable and inflexible arrangement. If you are a committed recording enthusiast a stand should be purchased as soon as possible. The gallows type is recommended above all others because it is so adaptable and in most cases will prove more satisfactory than the standard floor or table varieties. These have their uses but can be added to the basic equipment at a later date. If a number of stands are acquired over a period of time, ensure that all stands and microphone clips have compatible threads, or at least that suitable adaptors are available.

6. Organisation and method

In the remaining chapters we will discuss in some detail a variety of recording situations. The aim is to adapt or modify established professional recording techniques and operating procedures to meet the needs of the amateur. Recording, particularly the recording of drama, has very few rules. It is a fluid art form and provided one understands that the system has certain technical limitations, which govern the quality of a recording, almost anything is permissible. The more gifted the recordist the more he can bend the rules to his own convenience—even to the point of using the equipment incorrectly in order to produce a particular effect. This is justifiable provided either that you own the equipment which is being abused, or that you are confident it will not be damaged!

As far as the end product is concerned, what matters is the successful completion of the project and its critical acceptance. It is immaterial under what conditions it was made or how the equipment was used *provided* that the tape sounds right. It does not matter if an engineer tells you that what you propose to do is impossible or will not work satisfactorily, because he may not know the effect you are after. Try not to upset him, though, because you may be glad of his help if smoke comes pouring out of all the plug holes!

Preparation

Regardless of the type of recording session there are some matters of procedure which are essential and for the most part a matter of common sense. One obvious requirement is that there should be sufficient recording tape of a particular type to last for the length of the recording session. If this seems self-evident, ask any experienced recordist how often he has made a recording at the wrong speed. Anyone who has been used to a low speed machine will find tape being used up at an alarming rate at the higher speeds. This can be very embarrassing on a Sunday afternoon when the shops are closed. When recording in the village hall do check that you have chosen an evening when the Scouts are not meeting in an adjacent room. At home, make sure that your daughter is not having her young friends in to tea and that your wife is not proposing to go mad with the vacuum cleaner. Whether in the home or in some other location it is worth improvising a recording light outside the door to indicate when a 'take' is in progress. A darkroom type of lamp is quite distinctive and would probably serve well. Tradition has it that red lamps are used to indicate there is a recording in progress but if you should put one of these outside the front door you might be interrupted by unexpected visitors!

Other things to beware of are sounds which the ear takes for granted and discriminates against but which are all too apparent when the recording is replayed. A ticking clock is one example, but a stop watch can be equally obtrusive if placed on a table near

A A ticking clock in the recording room is a particularly annoying source of unwanted background noise.

B So is a stop watch if used in the vicinity of the microphone.

A

B

a microphone; the operation of its stop/start button also produces a sufficiently loud click to prove annoying. Sounds such as distant traffic or aircraft or next door's television are more difficult to deal with. It is important to monitor the recording continuously and if you become aware of extraneous noise break off recording, if at all possible, until the ambient noise has returned to its average level. If you ignore the noise and record come what may, the tape will be almost impossible to edit as the level of background noise will be bobbing up and down. The ideal edit is inaudible and the last thing you want is a dead give away, such as varying background noise, to draw attention to your 'skill'.

Atmosphere

Every recording, regardless of location, has an 'atmosphere'. In the case of a documentary this may be something instantly identifiable such as a background of dockyard activity. Alternatively, it may be the subtle 'breathing' of an apparently silent room. This is an indefinable type of background, yet totally distinctive, due partly to random air movement past the microphone in a particular environment, partly to structure-borne vibration and partly to electronic and tape noise. It is good practice to use bulk erased tape for all serious recording as this will have an inherently better S/N ratio than tape which is wiped by the machine's erase head. However, it should not be assumed that this bulk erased tape can be substituted for studio atmosphere. For this reason it is important to record a length of silence at the beginning and end of each recording, to capture the particular atmosphere of the recording location, or studio. This atmosphere will vary from day to day even in a given room and will also depend on the precise position of the microphone and on the settings of the various faders and tone controls.

Virtually every recording will require some sort of editing, and it is then that the atmosphere will be required. The silence which precedes the recording can generally be cut off and discarded unless it is being used to establish a mood or location, but it serves the very useful purpose of bringing the cast to order, ensuring they have finished shuffling feet, coughing and blowing noses. The atmosphere which trails the recording—about 30 s should be sufficient—should be carefully preserved and pieces of it used whenever a pause has to be lengthened during the editing. If anything else is used, whether blank tape or atmosphere from another room, it will not work.

Studio Procedure

The performers should be made aware at the beginning of a recording session what is required of them, and if the reason is explained to them they will co-operate readily. In particular warn them not to cheer, clap, laugh or cough until several seconds have elapsed after the end of a take, because the last words or last notes will die away naturally according to the reverberation time of the room. If anyone moves or makes a sound whilst this decay is occurring, it will spoil the whole effect which has been created. After these few seconds the cast can relax whilst you record the atmosphere. Coloured 'leader' tapes should be used to identify the beginning and end of each recording, or to separate one insert from another. It is advisable to adopt a colour convention: for instance yellow leader may be used to indicate the start of a recording and red leader the end. If there are a number of inserts on a single spool, white leader can be used to identify the individual inserts. Some types of leader tape can be written on with soft pencil or fibre tipped pen, and when recording drama it is helpful to number the various inserts so that the tape can quickly be married up with the script.

Cueing

Some sort of cueing system will be required, and this is particularly important if a separate cubicle is used for the technical equipment. All that is required is a simple signalling arrangement such as a lamp, battery and bell push. The idea is to place the light in a conspicuous position in the studio and to switch it on when you want to cue speech. If you want someone to speed up, flash the light quickly; if you want to reduce the pace, flash it slowly. But don't be surprised if your speaker loses his place and stops altogether! With a little ingenuity a simple code can be devised so that a speaker can be given basic instructions whilst recording.

Retakes

It is also important to have a set procedure for recording retakes. Generally it is better not to interrupt a speaker if he misreads a passage as, unless he is a very experienced performer, it may spoil the remainder of his recording. Mistakes should be marked in the script and retakes made at the end of the session, but these should never be done 'cold'. In order to get the speed, speech rhythm and intonation correct, the paragraph before the error should be recorded and at least a paragraph after it, allowing a choice of editing points. With a more experienced speaker the retakes can sometimes be done in sequence during the recording, as they become necessary, so that everything is more or less in its final order at the end of the session. The speaker should be told that if he makes a 'fluff' he must go back a paragraph and pick up the recording again in his own time. Wherever possible all the material from a particular speaker should be recorded at one session, as the atmosphere and performance are unlikely to be the same on separate days unless professional actors and facilities are used.

Script Layout

In discussing the recording of documentary, feature or drama material we presume that a script of some sort exists, or at least that there is a known framework into which the recording session fits. It is surprising how many amateur recording groups resent the work which is entailed in producing a workmanlike script. They seem to cherish a belief that enthusiasm and a headful of half-formed ideas will somehow be transformed into a work of art once the tape starts to roll. Unfortunately it seldom works that way. Musicians readily accept that there is little point in rehearsing without music, yet in other recording spheres the performers seem to regard a script as a necessary evil. Perhaps this is because everyone imagines he can write sparkling prose until he actually puts pen to paper!

It will probably be necessary to have a team effort to produce a script, or at least to assemble the bare bones of what is required. In a recording group there are usually one or two people who have some flair for writing and if pressed they will turn out a draft for discussion. As writers are notorious for leaving their work until the last minute it is advisable to set a deadline a week or so before you seriously expect to see any results. Once the script has been agreed it should then be written out in a way which is convenient for both actors and technicians. Ideally it should be typed and sufficient copies duplicated for each member of the team to have a personal copy which he can mark up in his own way.

The characters' names should appear in bold type to the left of the speech. Stage directions, sound effects and any non-dialogue information should be enclosed in brackets, underlined or typed differently to distinguish them from dialogue. Some experts prefer the instructions to be in the same column as the dialogue so that the eye scans them whilst reading the speech; others prefer all non-dialogue information to appear separately, in a column to the left of the dialogue.

Excerpt of a radio script from the pamphlet 'Writing for the BBC'.

MALCOLM:	What is it, darling?
EVE:	You know - when we were driving back this afternoon we passed someone on the road just before we got to the gates of High Woods....
MALCOLM:	I didn't notice.
EVE:	I know you didn't. You were all talking too hard. I only had a glimpse, because Langley was going pretty fast, but I had an idea that it was Gerald. Then I decided it was too much of a coincidence.
LANGLEY:	Well, it obviously was Gerald. What about it?
EVE:	Nothing. Only - he must have been coming from your house.
	(PAUSE)
MALCOLM:	Could he have been to see Minna?
LANGLEY:	(Slowly) He could - damn him!
	(FADE. FADE UP CAR DRAWING UP)
PHYLLIS:	You must be very pleased, Langley. It couldn't have gone better.
LANGLEY:	I am pleased.
	(CAR DOOR OPEN)
	I'll just put the car away. Phyllis - would you look after everyone? I expect you'd all like a drink before supper.
PHYLLIS:	Has Mrs Kent stayed late?
LANGLEY:	No - I told her not to. She'll have left us something cold before she went home to the village. I don't like anyone living-in here - when I come to the country I want to be on my own as far as possible - except for friends, of course...With you in a minute.
	(CAR DOORS SHUT. CAR MOVES OFF A LITTLE WAY, SLOWLY)
	(FOOTSTEPS ON GRAVEL)
PHYLLIS:	I've got a key.
	(DOOR OPENS)
	Oh the light's on! How careless of Mrs Kent. I'll leave the door for Langley . . . This way . . .
MACDONALD:	That was a very pleasant evening. A pity Minna didn't come.

Try to ensure that the script paper is of a type which does not rustle excessively when pages are turned. For this purpose the more absorbent type of duplicating paper is preferable to 'bond' typing paper. It is also worth arranging the script so that pages do not have to be turned in the middle of sentences: where possible they should be turned at the end of a speech. At times this may appear a little wasteful of paper as it may be necessary to leave part of the page blank, but script noise is such a bugbear when recording that anything which makes the performer's job easier is worthwhile. If possible, avoid clipping or stapling the pages of the script together as this frequently leads to rustling as the pages are turned. In most cases it will be more satisfactory to slide the pages across each other, putting the used pages to the back of the script rather than turning them. If a table is being used the pages can simply be placed out of the way as they are finished with.

The Recording Session

Recording sessions always seem to be too short and the available time passes far too quickly. Therefore it is important to start getting material on to tape as early as possible in the session. This means that all the preparation work should have been completed well in advance of the session and everyone should know exactly what he has to do. Ideally the members of the team who are responsible for the technical side should arrive before the cast so that the equipment is set up and tested by the time the performers are ready. Equally, the performers for their part should have rehearsed together before the recording session so that they are familiar with their parts. There should be no need for alterations to be made to the script at the last minute and no arguments about the exact wording of a particular passage. All these things should have been ironed out at the script conference and during the rehearsal. Once the recording session starts, the only rehearsal which takes place should be for the benefit of the technical staff, so that microphones can be adjusted and placed in the best positions. Voice levels can then be established, controls marked and any sound effects played so that everyone is familiar with them.

To avoid arguments as far as possible—and they are as prevalent amongst amateurs as professionals when a group of creative people get together—it is necessary for one person to be in charge of the operation: the producer. Some enthusiasts prefer to elect a different person to produce each project, others recognise that certain individuals have the gift of getting the best out of other people and are content to stick with a good producer when they have found one.

After the recording session, preferably on a separate day when everyone can listen objectively, the various takes should be played back and discussed by all concerned. It is only by being fiercely self-critical and listening to one's own work and comparing it with the best radio broadcasts that one's technique improves. Thus the craft of recording is developed: nothing that is written in a book will ever tell you how to get it right or even how to know when it is right. The old expression 'when it's right, it feels good' is absolutely true. One of the great enemies is complacency: no true artist is ever satisfied with his work.

Without something approaching professional pride in the end product you will turn out tapes that are as boring as the average holiday film. If more amateur cine enthusiasts would look at their work objectively they might understand why their friends edge away uneasily if they see the projector coming out. No one is interested in other people's failures, or family jokes that were funny two years ago. Do avoid at all costs letting an outsider hear your failures. The foregoing may seem to take the fun out of what is supposed to be a hobby, and of course there is no reason why a group of people should not get together when they feel like it and shout into a microphone. Anyone who enjoys recording should be given encouragement, but it must be recognised that a creative hobby is hard work, that there will be many disappointments and that unless a professional and to some extent disciplined approach is adopted, there will be a lot of frustration, wasted time and unnecessary failures. The purpose of this book is to encourage success, for success is the spur to talent.

Working Methods

If a recording session is to be successful it is important not only for you to be well organised but also to develop a consistent working method. No two people will tackle a particular recording project in exactly the same way and frequently there is no single correct answer to a particular problem. What there is, is a broad consensus of opinion amongst experienced recordists as to what constitutes a good recording engineer. Almost invariably in any discussion on the craft of recording, reference will be made to *touch*. Some people call it instinct, or 'driving by the seat of the

Use coloured pen or pencil to indicate changes of microphone and sound effects cues.

A

(SALOON CAR INTERIOR. CONTINUOUS)

TAPE 1
TRACK 1

HUGHES: Just keep on driving, Colonel. Unless you want a
            bullet through the head, that is.

COL: What kind of fool are you?

HUGHES: None. I know what I'm doing.

COL: There's no escape.

HUGHES: Not for you, maybe. For me there is. There's a plane
            waiting. (PAUSE) There's room for you - if you help me.

COL: Me? Help you? Never! You'll have to find your own
            way through that check point.

HUGHES: This way, then.

TAPE 2   (CLICK OF REVOLVER BEING COCKED. UNNATURALLY LOUD.)
            I've nothing to lose, Colonel. If you don't take me
            through, it's a bullet in the base of the spine for
            you and another through the brains for me. I'm sure we
            can do better than that.

COL: You wouldn't do either. I know the English.

HUGHES: You don't know me. Do you hear that noise?

TAPE 2   (RHYTHMIC SERIES OF THUDS AS THE TYRES HIT EVENLY-SPACED
            POT HOLES).

COL: So we don't have good roads!

HUGHES: Listen! It's speaking to you.....

TAPE 2   (THUD, THUD, THUD, THUD, THUD. SLOWLY FADE UNDER)

TAPE 1   .....It says: Die, die, die, die, DIE!
TRACK 2

B

ARMY CAMP

TAPE 2   (MARCHING. BARKED ORDERS. MEN DRILLING.) A TELEPHONE
            RINGS CLOSE TO MIC.)

DUTY OFFICER: Duty Officer. Just a minute. This confounded noise.

TAPE 2   (SASH WINDOW CLOSED. MARCHING FADES ABRUPTLY).
            What do you mean, disappeared. He left here over
            an hour ago. All right we'll check.

TAPE 2   (RINGS OFF. PHONE RINGS AGAIN IMMEDIATELY).

79

pants', or being at one with the equipment. And that is largely what it's all about: a good balance engineer has a great deal in common with a pilot, in that he must have absolute confidence in his machinery and must be able to operate it by an almost subconscious thought process, leaving his mind free to concentrate on the 'aerobatics' of the session.

An instance of this working method is the marking of a script. It is immaterial what convention you adopt provided the eye can scan the script and immediately understand the markings. When a number of microphones are in use it is helpful to identify these as 1,2,3,4 or A,B,C,D, and so on; inserts can be called GRAM 1, GRAM 2, TAPE 1, TAPE 2. Letters are preferable for mics and numbers for other equipment, as this helps to avoid confusion. For marking purposes coloured fibre-tipped pens are ideal, and every time there is a change of sound source this can be clearly indicated both by identifying the source, either by name or number. and by a change of colour (see page 79).

When recording popular music arranged for a large band a multimic set-up will be used and frequently the instrumental balance will be changing throughout the number, as different sections or soloists are featured. As it is very difficult to follow a score whilst controlling a musical balance, it is necessary either to have an assistant who can follow the score for you and call out the featured instruments, or to make yourself a 'lead' (or cue) sheet. One way of doing this is to make a chart representing the total number of bars in the tune, and to note at which bars the balance changes. The featured microphones can be indicated on the chart

A simple lead sheet for popular music can be made by representing the bars on a sheet of paper and indicating featured musicians, or changes of balance.

1 Piano intro	2	3	4
5 Full orchestra	6	7	8 +chorus
9	10	11	12
13 Sax riff	14	15	16 Drum solo (8 bars)

and provided you count the bars correctly, you will always be able to anticipate the change in balance and bring up the appropriate microphone(s). Some music balancers scoff at any form of note-making, cue sheets or score following and work entirely by feel. It is for the individual to find his own approach but it takes a great deal of experience to work by instinct alone.

When a number of microphones are employed it is easy to lose track of which mic is plugged to a particular channel. To simplify identification each mic stand should have a piece of adhesive tape stuck on it, labelled to show which instruments it is supposed to be covering. If the mixer channels carry similar information, say in Chinagraph above the channel fader, a great deal of time can be saved if a balance will not come together. Frequently it will be found that mic leads have been crossed somewhere and the required mic is not on the expected channel. With the aid of an assistant this can quickly be checked if the various sources are readily identifiable.

Phasing

Remember that microphones, like loudspeakers, must be correctly phased, and this is particularly true if they are to be used in close proximity. To test for phase, stand two microphones near together, set the gain control for each mic to the same level and ask someone, preferably male, to speak into them, standing so that he is 12–18 in (0.3–0.45 m) from each microphone. Whilst the person is speaking open and close one of the microphone faders and

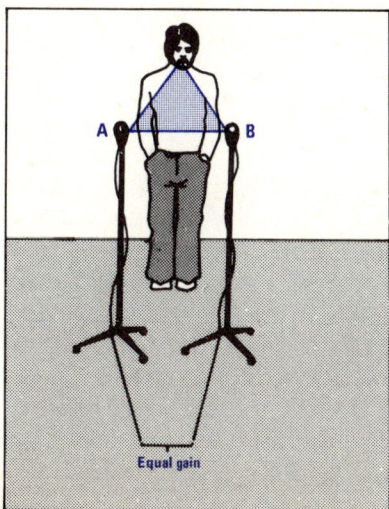

Equal gain

To phase microphones, test them in pairs with a speaker equi-distant from each microphone. If they are in phase the sound will be full-bodied; if they are out of phase the sound will be thin, lacking in bass.

81

notice if there is any change in speech quality. If the mics are out of phase the voice will sound thin or lacking in bass when both faders are open but the quality will improve as one fader is closed. If they are in phase there should be very little change in quality, provided, of course, they are both of a similar type. If more than two microphones are in use, A should be phased with B, then B with C and C with D and so on. If a mic is found to be out of phase its lead connections should be reversed or, in the case of a ribbon microphone only, it can be turned through 180°.

Coloration

Another problem encountered when several microphones are in use is that of coloration. This will be experienced when the same sound is picked up by more than one microphone, if the secondary mics produce an output of that sound which is of comparable level with that from the main mic. This problem can arise if, for example, there are two speakers A and B each with his own microphone a and b but if B's mic is left fully open while A is

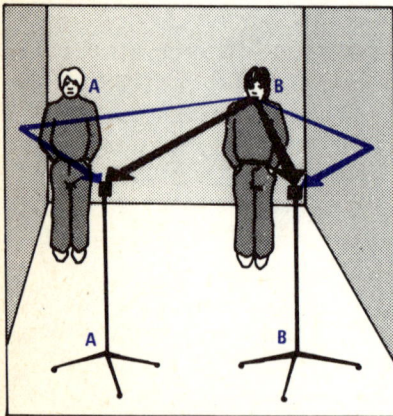

The sound quality will be degraded (coloured) if the same source is picked up on more than one microphone, if there is a high proportion of indirect (reflected) sound.

speaking, A will be picked up both by his own mic and, a fraction of a second later, by B's mic and the voice quality will be degraded. The same situation applies in reverse when B is speaking. In a larger discussion with more mics the problem is intensified. The answer is to use one's instinct and to 'ride' the microphone faders continually, partly closing faders which are not required. By following the discussion it is usually possible to divine who is likely to chip in next and to have the hand waiting on the fader. If you can see the faces of the contributors, watch for the tell-tale moistening of the lips or the eager opening of a mouth which indicates that speech is about to follow.

7. Drama and features

The most basic of all recording situations is that in which one person speaks into a microphone plugged directly to a tape machine. Under these conditions you could be forgiven for thinking that little could go wrong. In fact there are a number of quite simple errors which can be made, any one of which will spoil the quality of the end product. Some of these have been touched upon in earlier chapters: poor microphone technique, the use of an acoustically unsuitable room, obtrusive background noise, repeated hesitations, lack of fluency, bad technical operation resulting in tape overload or hiss.

What applies to a single individual working alone applies even more so to a group working as a team. The more sound sources and facilities used the more pitfalls there are to avoid. Therefore the situation of the solo recordist will not be specifically discussed, as much of what follows applies equally to 'one-off' or to team efforts. One point which should be made strongly is that there are very few people who can *ad lib* sufficiently fluently into a microphone to make an even passable recording. The only time a pure *ad lib* technique should be used is when recording a free discussion or an interview. On other occasions it is not always necessary or desirable to have a full script, but at least a few notes should be made so that the introduction, statement, linking narration, explanation or whatever have some form and follow a logical development. Most of us, unfortunately, communicate half-formed ideas in unfinished sentences, which is fine across the tea table but hardly inspiring when replayed on tape.

From a purely technical point of view, drama and feature recordings are approached in much the same way but from a production angle there are considerable differences of approach. For drama work it is important whenever possible to use actors with a fairly wide experience of amateur dramatics. As a general rule it is easier to train an actor in studio techniques than it is to turn a technical wizard into a fluent script reader. Apart from studio recordings, plays can of course be recorded live in the local hall during a performance. This will be discussed shortly, but under such conditions unwelcome technical compromises will inevitably have to be made.

Feature or documentary work can be approached in a variety of ways, one of the most common of which is to conduct a series of interviews with experts or interested parties and to intercut these with linking narration from a presenter. Usually people who are unfamiliar with recording will do better justice to themselves if they are interviewed in their own environment. An experienced voice is then only required for the narration.

Microphone Techniques

No matter how well produced a recording is, or how accomplished the actors, if the microphone technique is poor the whole effect will be marred. A microphone is a very delicate precision instrument and, by design, it is very sensitive to minor air movements. It will therefore not give of its best if used at very close range or if waved about at arm's length. There are exceptions to this: most of the excesses to which a microphone can be subjected are daily perpetrated by pop groups and at times the microphone even becomes integrated into the performance. For this type of application the appropriate type of microphone must be chosen with some care and it must be fitted with an efficient windshield. Masters of Ceremony are also major offenders in the use of microphones in that they invariably seem to shout too loud and to stand too near the microphone. The result is that the microphone 'pops' on plosive consonants, the overall sound level is too high and cannot be adequately controlled, and it suffers from severe overload distortion, rendering much of the speech unintelligible. For excitable close talkers such as commentators, specially designed microphones are available. One type is the lip ribbon microphone, which is not only ideal for close talking but has the added advantage that it discriminates against the ambient background noise, such as a large crowd.

When he is playing a role, it is easy for an actor inexperienced in the use of microphones to be carried away with his performance and to make the kinds of technical error already referred to. Ideally, as mentioned in an earlier chapter, the microphones should be mounted on robust floor stands. Each actor should work to his microphone and be discouraged from handling it, touching the stand or fiddling with the cable. When his part in a scene is over he should move quietly away from the microphone; if the floor is not carpeted, stockinged feet or slippers should be the order of the day.

One of the most useful microphones for drama work is the ribbon. It has several properties which can with advantage be used to make the performer's task more natural whilst producing the required effect. Because of the figure-of-eight polar diagram two or even four actors can work to one microphone, making possible face-to-face dialogue. Also, as we have seen, the ribbon mic

A Two or four actors can comfortably work to a single ribbon microphone. If two ribbons are used side-by-side, eight voices can be covered.

B If an actor moves to the side of a ribbon microphone, on a constant radius to it, he appears to recede into the middle distance.

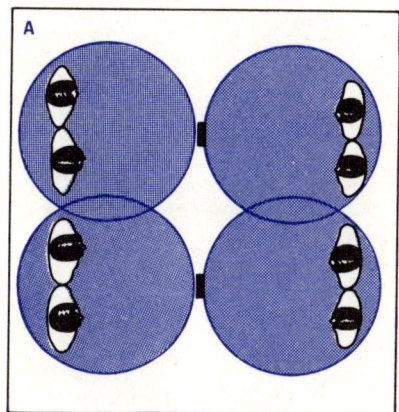

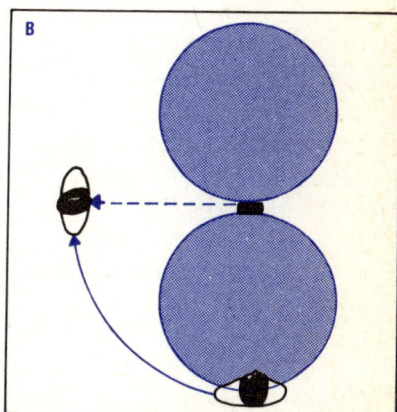

accentuates bass if used at a distance of about 6 in (15 cm), which can be turned to advantage. It tends to flatter male speaking voices and can be useful for narration: if addressed quietly at close range it gives a feeling of intimacy, or eavesdropping, or it can be used to create tension. Much depends on the context and on any accompanying effects. Another property of the figure-of-eight polar response is that if one moves to the side of the microphone, on a constant radius to it, one will appear to fade away into the middle distance. This is because the lobes of sensitivity are to the front and back of the ribbon and as the actor moves sideways out of the lobe he appears, subjectively, to have receded from the listener. This will not be so noticeable or effective in a live room where multiple reflections undermine the directional properties of the microphone.

Suggesting Environment

In addition to the properties of the microphone itself, there are other means of suggesting environment, the most obvious of which is to add echo to the voice. But remember, echo implies space and hard reflecting surfaces. It is the blunt instrument of prison cell atmosphere and of caves; it should never be used on outdoor scenes. On music it must be applied with understanding and discretion (see Chapter 8). To create the effect of the distant end of a telephone conversation, try using a carbon or crystal microphone in conjunction with a degree of bass and treble filtering to simulate the restricted frequency range of a telephone circuit. If an old telephone handset is available this will do well, but a bell battery will be required to supply a standing d.c. voltage.

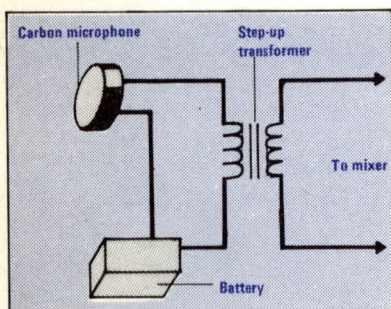

A carbon microphone from an old telephone can be useful for simulating one end of a telephone conversation. A bell battery and a transformer will be required, as shown.

Frequently a particular environment will be sufficiently well suggested by establishing sound effects, but at times something more is required and some improvisation is called for. Possibly the combination of a particular microphone in a specific recording location, such as a cloakroom or corridor or a backstage cubby hole at the village hall, will be called for. It is worth trying to arrange the loan of a good quality portable machine for recording items away from the main studio base. If all else fails a good cassette recorder *may* give satisfactory results provided that the tape is later copied to an open reel system and properly edited

86

and assembled as an insert tape. These non-studio scenes should be kept as few as possible and should be recorded in advance of the main recording session, so that they can be played into the recording in sequence.

When gaining experience of what can be done with a given microphone in a given acoustic it is a good idea to gather a few friends together for the odd evening, just for an experimental session. Try using different microphones in various parts of the hall—say in the centre of the floor, in an alcove or closely surrounded by drapes—and observe the effect of speaking at different distances from them. In particular try to arrange to have

By furnishing or stripping an area of a hall, differing acoustics can be created to suggest particular environments.

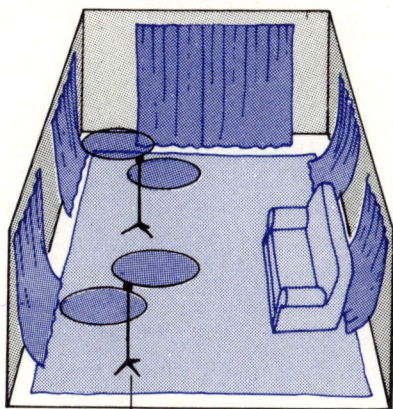

Two ribbon microphones

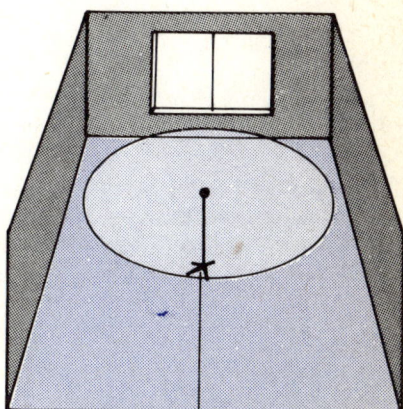

One omnidirectional microphone

one end of the room curtained and partially carpeted and filled with as much soft clutter as possible. The other end should be given the opposite treatment and virtually stripped bare. You will find that you have created two apparently entirely different locations, one of which might reasonably pass as a luxury flat whilst the other would be nearer to a warehouse.

Sound Perspective

As far as pure technique is concerned it is important that unless a vocal effect of some kind is intended, the actor should try to maintain a constant distance between his mouth and his microphone. Any sudden, unexpected movement will give a change of sound perspective, a change of quality and a major change of level. It may also produce distortion due to overload of the microphone, preamplifier or the tape itself. Sound perspective is something which is achieved not by one person speaking quieter or louder than another, or by the control of voice levels with the mixer. It is a matter of the ratio of direct to indirect (or reflected) sound picked up by a microphone, and so is similar

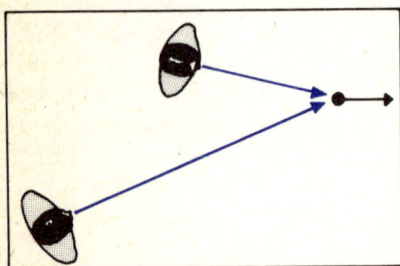

Sound perspective gives the impression of depth and is not a matter of differing voice levels but of physical distance from the microphone. This changes the ratio of direct to indirect sound received by the microphone.

to the earlier example of someone walking to the side of a ribbon microphone. However, it can be used in more subtle ways, requiring just a change of weight from one foot to another, a minor head movement or a lean away from the mic. For example, in an interrogation or a battle of wits where the initiative is passing from one character to another, if the sound perspective follows the changing moods it can heighten the drama. This sort of thing must not be overdone and largely it should go unnoticed by the average listener. It is one of those professional touches which goes to make the whole greater than the sum of its parts.

It is also important to remember when casting a sound drama that the listener will form his own images of place and appearance. It does not matter if all the men are one-legged, bald, corpulent and twenty-two years old and the women all look like Charley's Aunt, provided they have individual voices. Vocal texture is of immense importance and each character should be immediately identifiable. If you are using a published script by a good dramatist, the dialogue will give the characters an identity. If you are writing your own script try—it is a very specialised art—to give each character an individual speech rhythm.

Sound Effects

Sound drama leans heavily on the use of effects, but they must be used with care. Frequently they need not be specific or exact, or even true to life. What matters is not so much the particular noise of a sound effect, as its suggestive influence on the listener in the context of the particular drama. This is an important point: the listener should be led to envisage a three-dimensional scene for himself and he should not have your version of that scene too enthusiastically thrust down his throat! At the same time there are occasions when one must be specific: bird song and animal sounds are obvious examples. The right creature must be in the right location in the right season. Similarly with transport— vehicles have their own distinctive sounds and a lorry cannot readily be substituted for a double decker bus.

We can broadly divide sound effects into two types. Firstly, there are long running background effects which establish the mood of a scene or set a location. Effects of this kind are referred to as *atmospheres*. Secondly, there are short duration effects, known as *spot* effects, such as closing doors, pistol shots, breaking glass and so on. (Incidentally, on scripts the abbreviation FX is often used for 'effects'.) It is not usually necessary to record the more common types of atmosphere or spot effect as most of these are now available on commercially released long playing records. Given a turntable with a reasonably quick start and a pickup which it is easy to cue accurately, it is feasible to play the atmosphere direct from the effects record, but there are good reasons for not doing so. Many of the commercially available atmospheres are of quite limited duration and have to be extended by repeated copying to make them last for the length of a scene. This technique is discussed in Chapter 9. Also a record has a limited life in this application and it makes economic sense to copy the required sound on to tape and preserve the record in as good a condition as possible for use on future occasions. Another consideration is that few domestic turntables, even if modified, will give the kind of precise start to an effect which is required for drama; even a quite modest recorder will probably prove to be more convenient in this respect.

Practical Considerations

A practical recording set-up in a village hall could be equipped on the following lines. The studio has the live and dead ends already discussed, and is equipped with a variety of microphones. In the control room there is a mixing desk, with monitoring either by loudspeaker or headphones, a high quality record/replay machine on to which the final production is assembled, two insert (replay) machines—for playing sound effects, pre-recorded speeches or music into the studio material—and one or two gram decks used either for playing direct or for dubbing purposes, as already described.

Possible recording arrangements, A, in a village hall and B, in a living room.

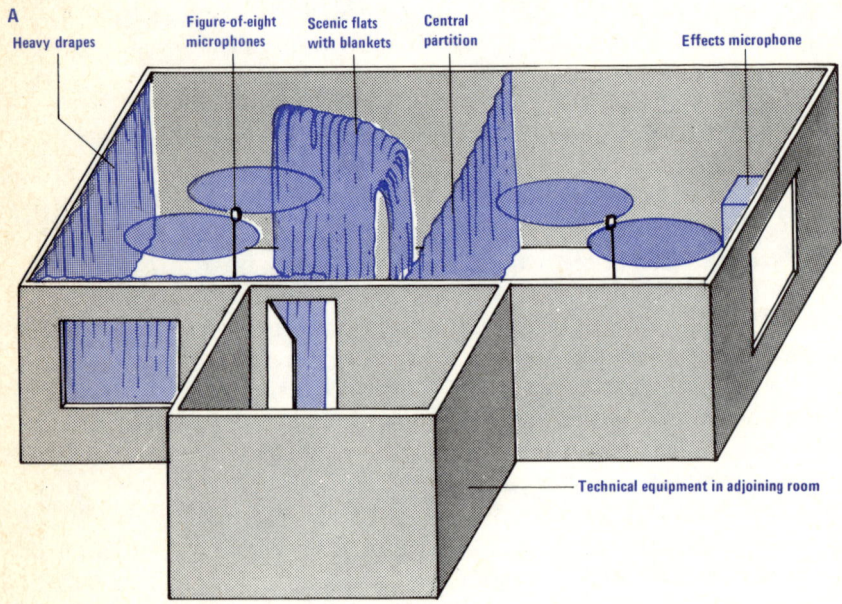

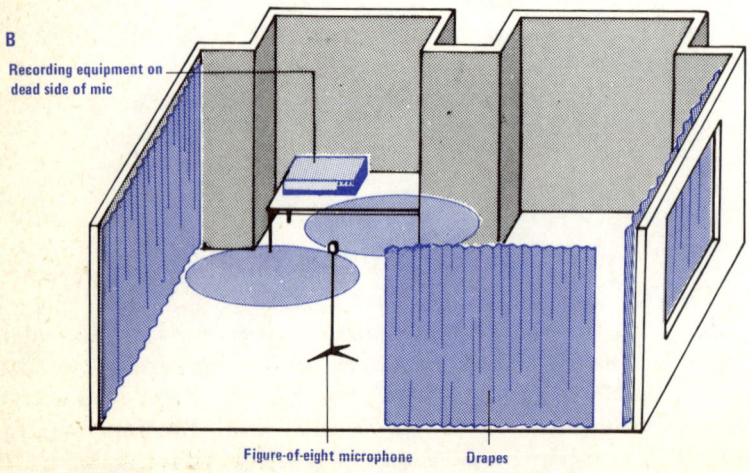

A

Heavy drapes

Figure-of-eight microphones

Scenic flats with blankets

Central partition

Effects microphone

Technical equipment in adjoining room

B

Recording equipment on dead side of mic

Figure-of-eight microphone

Drapes

In a typical recording session the sequence of events would be rather like this. Once the script has been produced in an acceptable form, the cast rehearse their roles with the producer. The technicians study the script and decide what facilities will be required to put over the drama and create a convincing sound picture. Effects sequences will be made up either by lifting tracks from records or by specifically recording more obscure material. Some of the speeches may also have to be recorded if a particular dramatic effect is required or if it has to be precisely timed either with other narration or with spot effects. Where possible it is advisable to assemble all the spot effects material on to one spool with each separate cue clearly identified and referenced to the script with a numbered leader tape. The other tape machine will have the long running atmospheres, and the gram decks will only be used live on occasions when there is insufficient time to spool the insert machines through to the next cue. This is a technique which comes with practice. During rehearsal it will become clear where effects have to be juggled from one piece of equipment to another to make the technical operation run smoothly.

Ideally there will be a two-man team at the recording and balancing end, plus the producer, with one man looking after the sound-mixing operations and running the record machine. The other man is responsible for the preparation and cueing of all tape inserts and sound effects. If the record machine is considerably superior in quality to the ones used for the inserts, it makes sense to record the effects on the main machine and to use the insert machine(s) for replay purposes only.

In television and the cinema, atmospheres tend to run throughout a scene. In sound drama it is more usual to establish the scene and then gradually to fade the effects behind the dialogue. The atmosphere is then re-established towards the end of a scene to give a transition to a new location. Much depends on the context and there will be times when it will be essential to have atmosphere running throughout a scene.

Montages and Loops

It often happens that the particular effect you want to use does not exist. This is particularly true when trying to create the atmosphere of a specific time or place. One of our favourite examples of this kind of technique is the scene in *Vanity Fair* when the British troops are marshalling in Brussells on the eve of

Waterloo. As they did so before the tape recorder was invented we have to imagine the scene, with the help of Mr Thackeray, and build a sound picture or montage which conveys the spirit of the scene. Accuracy is not essential, we simply have to feed the mind with an idea; the dialogue will do the rest. What do we need? Fife and drum music for the men to march to; sounds of marching, shouted commands, crowds cheering, cavalry and horse drawn carriages. What do we use? A commercially available fife and drum record, an effects record of the British army (modern) marching at 120 paces per minute—no matter that Wellington's men were not so well shod nor striding down metalled roads. If we mix these together, with the music and marching fading in and out, giving the impression of a continuous muster, we have established part of the picture. Crowds, horses, carriages, shouting. What does that remind one of? The Coronation? A State Occasion? Princess Anne's Wedding? Exactly. Select a few bits from the record of the event, join them together on tape, mix them over what you already have, and you've created something new. A similar technique could be used to build a montage of an air raid or a futuristic factory.

At the other extreme, one sometimes has to create loneliness or silence. Here a sound is needed which emphasises the quietness of the location: something which normally would be inaudible. Perhaps a watch ticking, a slow drip of water in a cave, a cricket chirping, a foot scraping on a floorboard. An effect such as dripping water or the ticking watch may have to run for a considerable time, possibly throughout a scene, and the best way of doing this—as with any repetitive sound—is to make a tape loop. The idea is to record a short length of the effect and then to form a section of it into an endless loop. A little practice will be

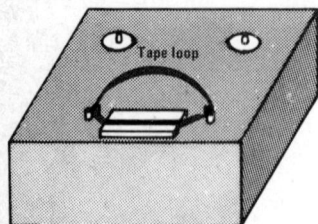

A tape loop can be used to give a continuous sound effect. Further details are given in Chapter 9.

required to make a join which is inaudible. The important things are that there is no change in level either side of the join and that the repetitive rhythm of the effect is exactly maintained. If a long loop is used it will need weighting—a patch cord is ideal—to maintain tension on the tape. This and other specialised editing techniques are dealt with in Chapter 9.

'Practical' Effects

Apart from pre-recorded sound effects, there are others which are better done live in the studio using so-called 'practical' equipment. This could be dishes in a bowl of water, accompanied by much splashing, or a bolt being drawn dramatically. Effects of the latter type are often more convincing and better synchronised to the action if performed in view of the actors. If a reasonably sized hall is used, a separate microphone should be set up for these live spot effects. It is very useful to have available a board which will creak, a miniature door with a number of different types of lock, a selection of doorbells, a noisy hinge and a tarpaulin. If the tarpaulin is spread on the floor and a few bucketsful of gravel are poured over it, a couple of enthusiastic walkers can produce magnificent footstep effects: you can almost smell the fog and Mr Hyde!

Cueing

During the recording it is important that the actors can hear the effects which are used, and these should be fed at low level to a loudspeaker in the studio. This is known as *foldback* and it is important to set the level carefully during rehearsal, firstly because of the danger of acoustic feedback or 'howl-round', and secondly because even below the howl threshold, the studio mics will pick up the foldback and the result will be coloration, giving the sound a muddy quality. If space or technical facilities are limited, it may not be possible to provide foldback, in which case the actors will have to take visual cues or else wear headphones fed with just the effects channel from the mixer.

The use of effects and the cueing of insert tapes is an acquired art. There are two aspects to this art: one is maintaining the correct balance between the dialogue and any accompanying music or effects; the other is anticipating the moment at which to start the tape, so that the effect is heard at exactly the right point in the action. In the case of spot effects, an instant start using the pause button is probably the answer, but with an effect which builds up, such as a car arriving, this will have to be started in advance and timed against the dialogue so that the final scrunch of tyres on

93

gravel occurs just as Sir Percy says, 'My God! It's Carruthers,' or some other gem of equal literary merit.

Sound Balance

As for the matter of sound balance, this is something which cannot be taught: it has to be felt. It is important to bear in mind the likely monitoring level when the tape is replayed, because if you monitor at a level greatly different from this a different subjective impression of the balance will be obtained. Effects must be loud enough to register but they should not be obtrusive or larger than life unless dramatic licence demands otherwise. If the replay level is considerably lower than the monitoring level, effects which sounded correct will tend to be inaudible. As far as speech is concerned, most amateur actors seem to drive the first few syllables of each sentence harder than the rest and these staccato bursts of high level speech can give rise to overload distortion. The only answer is anticipation and a slight easing down of the fader during sentence pauses. If an actor is a particularly bad offender, he may be able to give a more controlled delivery if he is made aware of the problem. One of the difficulties

The dynamic range of the programme material exceeds that which can be accommodated on tape. To avoid overload on one hand and tape hiss on the other, the fader levels are adjusted in anticipation of quiet and loud passages. The dynamic range is thus compressed but the sound retains dramatic impact.

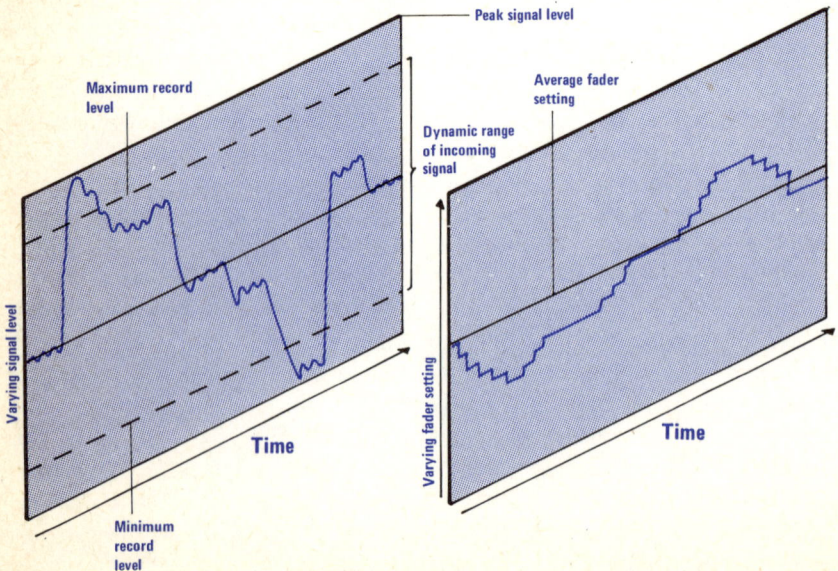

94

and one of the arts of sound balancing is containing the wide dynamic range of speech encountered in drama, within that which can technically be accommodated. Ear, eye and hand must work closely together and the level must be controlled in sympathy with the dramatic feel of the production. A similar approach is also adopted with music: a mean modulation level is established and when a loud passage is anticipated, the level is dropped in progressive stages—by pulling back the fader—so that when the climax comes there is sufficient 'headroom' to accommodate it without producing tape overload. The same technique applies to quiet passages: here the mean level is gradually raised so that when the quiet passage comes it is within the acceptable dynamic range of the recorder and not lost in the system noise.

Live Drama

Before leaving the subject of drama, we should perhaps consider how to approach the recording of a play during a live performance on stage. The easy answer, of course, is don't. Wherever possible get the cast together and record the play for posterity as an entirely separate project. If you want to capture the atmosphere of a live performance, record the audience reaction one evening in the theatre and dub this on to the recording as appropriate. If you really do want to do it the hard way, it will be necessary to suspend a number of microphones over the stage area. In order to get these into the right positions it will be necessary to attend several rehearsals and plot on a stage plan the areas where significant dialogue occurs. It will not be possible or

A If a stage performance is to be recorded, it is essential to attend rehearsals and to plot the actors' positions on a floor plan. If possible a rehearsal should be recorded to establish sound levels.

B Microphones can be slung over the stage area and supplemented by stand mics in the orchestra pit.

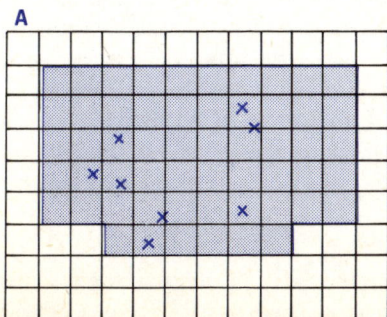

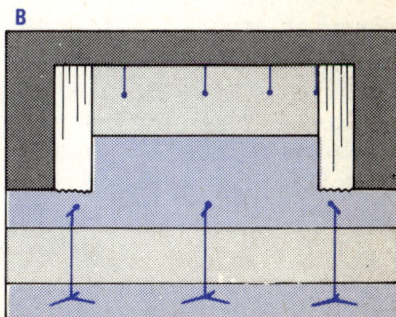

practicable to saturate the stage with microphones, and some degree of sound quality will have to be sacrificed, particularly on throw-away lines. If much of the action is played down-stage and direct to the audience, further mics will be required in the pit area. These should be on floor stands, extended sufficiently for the microphones to protrude above the footlights. Obviously the higher the microphones can be positioned the better, but it is important not to interfere with the audience's view of the stage. Inevitably the sound will be lacking in presence and, because of the distant microphone technique adopted, it will have an open or coloured quality. If the recording is a particularly important one it is worth investigating the economics of hiring a pair of highly directional *rifle* microphones for the occasion. These

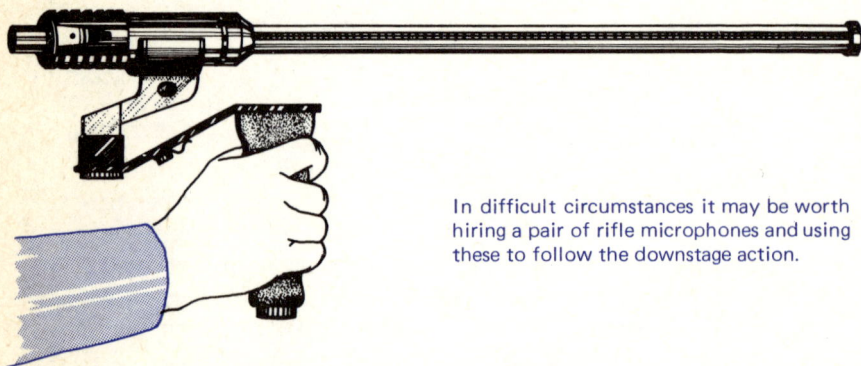

In difficult circumstances it may be worth hiring a pair of rifle microphones and using these to follow the downstage action.

would then be supplemented by the fixed stage mics as required. Each mic requires an operator, who follows the action much as a sniper follows his target, and he should be able to hear the output of the mixer on headphones.

If possible, try to avoid recording any material, such as spot effects or announcements, which come from the theatre's P.A. system. It is advisable to use a little dramatic licence here—perhaps without informing the cast!—and to edit in the effects afterwards, wherever practicable. Anything picked up from the theatre P.A. system via a stage mic will in all probability be of apalling quality and there will be no way of controlling the level of the effects except by fading down the stage mics—which could prove embarrassing.

Finally, if you enjoy projects of this nature and are good at producing creative sound effects, you will probably be welcomed with open arms at the local amateur drama group. It is a good way of gaining valuable experience and at the same time making useful contacts for future recording work.

Features

Many of the techniques which have been discussed in this chapter can be applied equally to the making of feature tapes. However, features are a different version of the art and a different approach is called for. On the technical side it is usually possible to make do with much more basic facilities and, as with filming, bring the subject to life on the editing bench. With regard to production, there are a number of approaches which can be adopted. There may be no narration at all, no presenter, no editorial voice, simply the various interviewees making their own points in their own ways. To maintain pace and interest no single voice should be allowed to continue for too long, and comments from different interviews should be juxtaposed. Even at the amateur level, the professional ethic should be observed that no matter how much an interview is edited it should (a) fairly represent the point of view of that individual, and (b) not be deliberately cut in such a way as to make a fool of the speaker. If you wish to use something for a humorous effect, permission should be sought from the person concerned.

Alternatively a subject may be introduced by a studio narrator and the theme developed by the above interview technique, with the subjects being interviewed in their home environment if possible. Any editorial points will then be made in the linking narration. If there is a great deal of studio narration, more than one voice should be used to give some light and shade to the sound picture. It is important to make use of vocal texture as much as possible— these are the oils with which you paint—and to find speakers who are easy on the ear.

Sometimes a number of interested parties can be assembled in the studio on a type of *Any Questions* basis. The ensuing free discussion is then allowed to run its course and the relevant points edited together afterwards. Generally, a subject will suggest the approach which is adopted and the important thing is not to be afraid to experiment or to innovate. In the early days in particular, listen to broadcast documentaries and take note of the various techniques adopted.

A feature may not need such a rigid script as a drama but it must be taut and free from waffle. Remember you are continually fighting for the listener's attention, and if that listener is a competition judge, you cannot afford to lose his interest! Having produced a draft script, record and edit the interviews, then start to polish the linking narration and effects. You may find you are telling a very different story from the one originally envisaged. Try to begin with an intriguing effect or an interesting remark so that curiosity is immediately aroused and thereafter keep the story moving along. Do not be tempted to equate quality with quantity: padding is unnecessary and if the natural length of the feature is less than you had intended, if it sounds right, leave it alone.

Interviews

Interviewing is a very special craft and a very difficult one to master. One of the important things to remember is that the interviewer is unimportant, his personality should not dominate proceedings and he should not inhibit the interviewee from making his point. A good interviewer is a good listener: he must try to have a personal interest in what is being said and to lead the conversation in the general direction the subject of the feature demands. Try not to interrupt a train of thought but only to prompt. On many a television interview you will notice that a second question is asked before the first is answered, with a result that the viewer is irritated by getting half-answers to both questions. Again, if your interviews are to be edited and intercut with a number of others, it is important to be able to cut out the interviewer's voice entirely in some cases. Having asked a question, let the answer come in its own time. Don't keep saying, 'Yes' or 'No' or muttering, or you will regret it later, as your voice will always be just where you would like to make a cut. Encourage the speaker with nods, smiles and gestures, preferably having explained beforehand what you intend to do.

It is a good idea to have a list of questions you would like to ask, and these are particularly useful if you encounter someone who is slow to warm to his subject. But do not spoil your opportunities and slavishly work through a list of questions regardless of the answers which are elicited. An interview is a living thing; it has a habit of developing in its own way into something unexpected. Be aware of what is happening, of what this person is saying, and if his answer suggests another question or another sphere of interest, another line of enquiry, forget your prepared list and let flesh and blood take over. This is what recording is all about.

Mostly, as has been said, interviews of this type will be conducted on location, but use a little discretion about where you record. A noisy playground or a major trunk road may have the right atmosphere but if what the person says is lost behind the background noise, it is of little value. Effects can always be added later, to suggest location if the recording seems too dead, but do not overdo it. With drama the effects are often used to exaggerate reality; with documentary they underline it. It's an interesting tightrope to walk, but one that grows wider with experience.

8. Music

Before discussing specific techniques it is worth considering, briefly, the development of music recording. The birth of broadcasting and the advent of talking pictures were two events which introduced the sound medium to a very wide public. Recording then was a very crude operation and one more allied to mechanical than to electronic engineering. Everything was in mono, of course, and there were no tape recorders, so each take had to be a direct, effectively live, recording on to wax. Wax preceded the use of lacquer for the cutting of record 'masters'. In the event of a mistake the entire piece had to be repeated. Working under this form of constraint, the film and record companies established simple and effective techniques of sound balancing. Frequently a single microphone was used and the musicians were shuffled around until the sound balancer liked what he heard; then a take was made, and this could only last for around five minutes as this was as much as could be accommodated on a commercial 12in 78r.p.m. record.

Soon microphones were improved and electronic mixers began to appear; it was then possible to produce an enhanced sound texture. That is, individual microphones gathered only part of

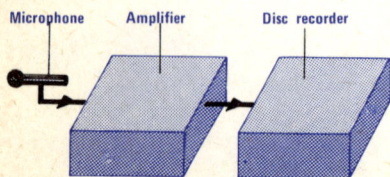

Microphone   Amplifier   Disc recorder

In the early days of recording each take was a direct, effectively live, recording on to wax.

100

the sound picture and these had to be blended to produce a recognisable end product. The sound balancer now became a very powerful part of the recording team and was able to create a type of sound which would be impossible in the concert hall. The importance of certain instruments could be exaggerated, a melody line could be carried by an instrument which would normally have been swamped by the brass and rhythm sections.

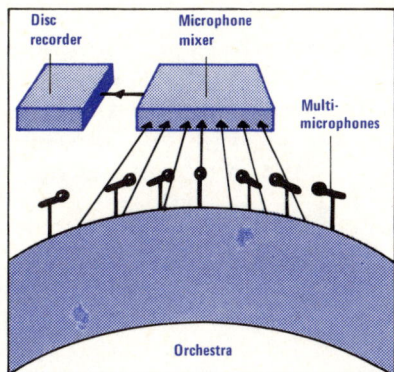

As techniques and equipment improved, increasing numbers of microphones were used to gather the orchestral sound.

In this period of rapid development, the big band was in its heyday and men like Glenn Miller were pioneering whole new concepts in musical texture. The art of recording grew ever more complex and refined, but Miller, who was a man of strong character and a dedicated bandleader, had no time for multiple microphone set-ups and he insisted on presenting a balanced sound to a single microphone. He would spend a great deal of time at a session moving the musicians, until the sound began to come together. What he achieved was unique in dance band music and his recordings are a living proof that light orchestral arrangements can be successfully recorded using the most basic microphone techniques.

Multi-or Single-mic?

Thus there were different schools of thought about sound balancing and the controversy was later fired by the introduction of the multitrack tape recorder into the studios, allowing an insensitive sound balancer to commit the grossest atrocities on an innocent piece of music. Classical music was not untouched by all this. In the beginning a single microphone, somewhere above the 101 conductor's head, was used. This became a crossed pair for early stereo recordings, but many balancers and record producers felt the need to improve on the natural thing and additional microphones were used, which gave a degree of presence and brilliance to classical recordings which had not been heard before. Nor was it universally approved of, and even today many critics maintain that some of the most satisfying stereo recordings are those made using the crossed pair configuration introduced by Alan Blumlein.

Today's amateur cannot hope to compete with a fully equipped multitrack studio. Nevertheless he can produce excellent recordings, based on simple techniques, which will bear comparison with those made using the most complex equipment. The important thing is to recognise your limitations, both in

For stereo the single microphone becomes a crossed pair. The microphones should have a figure-of-eight or a cardioid characteristic.

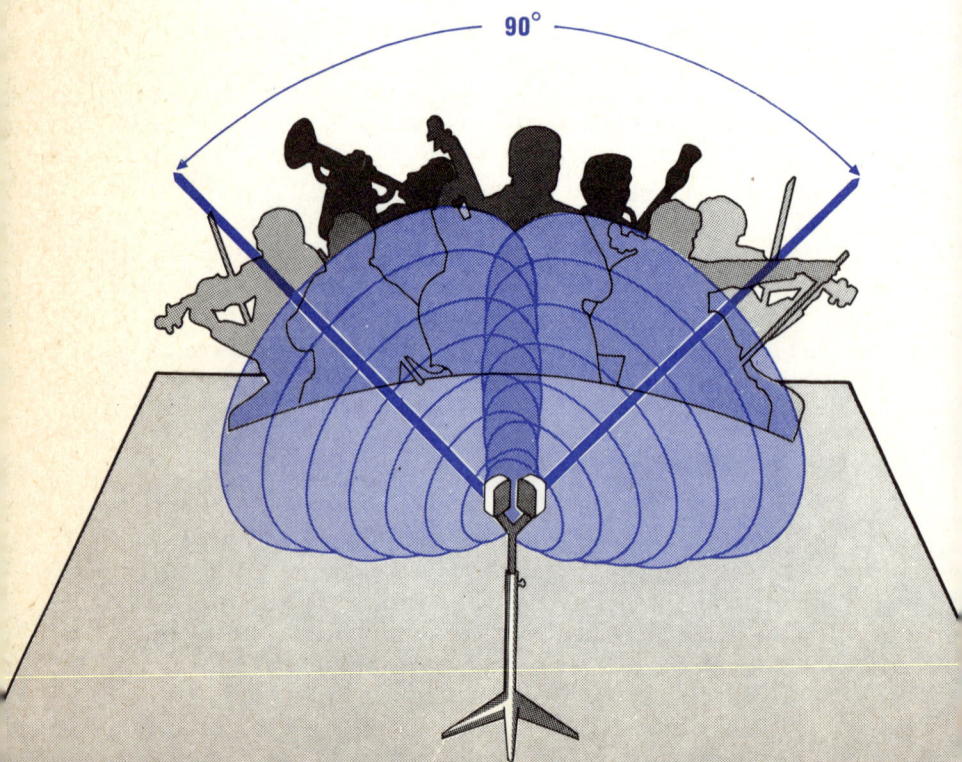

terms of experience and facilities. The limitation of experience will be overcome by time and application; the limitation of facilities by an intelligent selection of repertoire to record.

Balance Techniques

To an extent, music recording is a process of trial and error: the important thing is to recognise the truth when it is arrived at. One moment the balance will be wrong, the next it will begin to 'come together'. A series of subtle changes will be necessary but an instant will come when you know it is right. The difference may be just a minor re-positioning of a microphone, a fraction more level from one instrument or the use of a screen to prevent the drum sound from spilling on to other microphones. The basic techniques can be learned, but the ability to recognise truth cannot—it is largely an inherent talent. What it amounts to is the ability to carry a sound in the head and to know, instinctively, when you have created that sound and are in a position to record it. There are no absolutes in this craft, no fixed points of reference—each session has its own version of truth. Phase Four Stereo is one; Neville Marriner and the Academy of St. Martins is another. Both are correct but they are not interchangeable. You must know which you want and only the ear will tell you when you have found it.

In essence recording consists of two skills. One is the placing of microphones and the arrangement of the studio to allow a satisfactory mix to be obtained, and the other is the balance and control of the incoming musical information.

Mic Placing

The only thing which counts when placing a microphone is that it picks up the sound you want and produces the effect you are after.

We have already mentioned that early orchestral recordings were made using a single microphone and that many stereo recordings have been made using a simple crossed pair of microphones. A great many people maintain that this is still the best way to record a classical orchestra. They say that the orchestra has a natural internal balance which will be arrived at by the conductor, who will rehearse until he is satisfied with both the interpretation and the musical texture. The main art then for the sound balancer is to find a position for the microphone where it will faithfully 103 reproduce the balance which is perceived by the conductor with his ears. This is no easy thing, because the hearing mechanism is complex, and the conductor's brain is compensating for deficiencies caused by the acoustic environment. The microphone may pick up the same overall sound but it cannot process it in the way that the brain does, before committing the sound to tape. When the tape is replayed the brain will not be able to compensate for any deficiencies which exist: rather it will become increasingly irritated by the flaws and consequently more harshly critical of the musical performance than it would be in a concert hall.

This is not to say that we do not believe in a single-microphone technique—we do, if the conditions are right. The main problem for the amateur is that he will frequently be working under conditions which the professional would say were acoustically impossible. Under these circumstances it is likely that no single microphone position will be adequate and that additional, so-called *spot* microphones, will be required to reinforce some sections of the orchestra, or to bring out a solo passage.

The best initial approach is to sling the main microphone some 10–15 ft (3.0–4.5 m) above and behind the conductor, and looking down towards the orchestra at an angle of about 45°. Thereafter a great deal of patience and trial and error are required to find an optimum position which presents a well balanced sound to the microphone. If a number of works by different composers are being recorded it is likely that each work will require a re-positioning of the microphone. Everything depends on the tonal balance of the composition, its musical texture and dynamic range, and the relative importance of the instrumental groups. No instrument or group of instruments should dominate another and in particular the brass should not overshadow the strings.

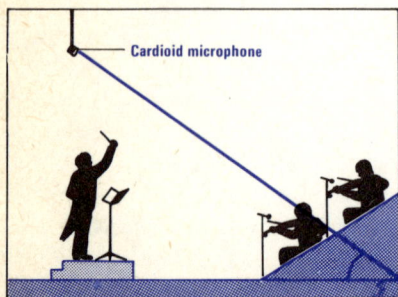

Cardioid microphone

The acoustics of many halls are not satisfactory for a single-microphone technique. A cardioid microphone some 10–15 ft (3.0–4.6 m) above the conductor's head, usually biased towards the string section, is used for the overall balance. Additional 'spot' microphones are used for extra definition.

Spot Microphones

Unless a very good hall is available it is unlikely that a single microphone position will be satisfactory. In all probability some solo passages, accompanying rhythms, subdued melodies and odd instruments such as the triangle will be barely audible although the overall orchestral sound is good. The unsatisfactory areas are then reinforced with spot microphones which are mixed in as required to improve the overall texture. When filling out the sound in this way it is important not to go too close with the spot mics or the orchestral perspective will be lost. If a stereo recording is being made, the *pan-pot** on the mixer should be used to position the sound from the spot mic so that it occupies the correct position on the stereo stage.

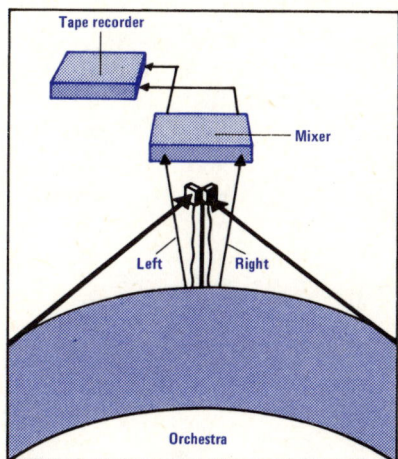

The output of the crossed pair is fed through the mixer to the record machine. Left and right channels remain completely separate.

In a simple stereo recording set-up with a crossed pair of cardioid microphones providing left and right information, the microphones could be fed direct to a stereo tape recorder but, as was mentioned in Chapter 4, it is better to control the sound through a mixer. In the present example the mixer should have group outputs to feed the left and right channels of the tape recorder. The fader for one microphone is then switched to the left group whilst the other is switched to the right. Once the overall orchestral texture is satisfactory the stereo stage can be manipulated to some extent by the relative levels of the two

*A pan-pot is a fader supplementary to the channel fader which determines what proportion of the output of that channel is fed to the left and right groups. According to these ratios a sound can be placed anywhere from extreme left, through centre to extreme right. If all pan-pots were set to centre, a mono recording would result.

microphone faders. If additional spot mics are used and the mixer does not have pan-pot facilities, each microphone should be fed to two channels. To do this an adaptor lead should be made up. If one channel is fed to the left group and the other to the right, then by varying the relative settings of the two faders, the source can effectively be pan potted across the stereo stage.

Opera

Operatic works present considerable problems to the amateur. In addition to capturing a good orchestral sound, which at times is merely accompaniment and at others is a powerful dramatic or melodic force, he has to balance it against the full dynamic range of an opera singer or the harmony of a choir. The problem is one of containment: in the quietest aria the voice must not be lost in the orchestra, at the same time the level of the vocal mic cannot be greatly increased, otherwise it will pick up too much of the orchestra and degrade the sound quality. In stereo it will also destroy the spatial effect. The microphone therefore cannot be too distant from the singers; nor must it be too close to them or the vocal perspective will be wrong and there will probably be overload distortion in the microphone amplifier or on tape.

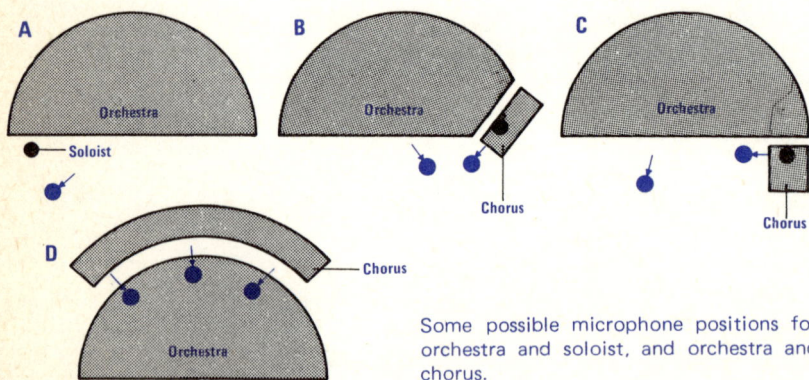

Some possible microphone positions for orchestra and soloist, and orchestra and chorus.

If the recording is not taking place during a live performance it is possible to adjust the position of the singer relative to both the orchestra and the microphone until a satisfactory balance is obtained. If the performance is done to a live audience then it is essential to attend a dress rehearsal. Infinite patience must then be exercised placing and adjusting microphones until you are certain you have established the best obtainable balance under the circumstances.

106

Choral Works

Large choral works present much the same problems as opera, but there is an additional problem in that choral music above all is a severe test for distortion arising through *intermodulation*. As the name implies, intermodulation distortion is caused by one frequency reacting with another to produce an unwanted output signal which was not present at the input. Choral music is rich in harmonics and it also presents to the microphone a large number of voices all nominally singing the same note but in fact drifting above and below the exact frequency of that note. Thus the whole programme chain, from microphone through amplifier and tape to loudspeaker, is being subjected to a severe intermodulation distortion test. Therefore, if this type of recording is to be done successfully it is necessary to use equipment of a high enough performance standard to minimise this problem.

Light Music

Light orchestral music, modern jazz and big band arrangements call for a different approach. We have already seen that in the early days microphone set-ups were quite basic, and it was customary to shuffle players around as necessary to produce a well balanced sound. Glenn Miller was cited as an example of this approach to recording. Given the right type of arrangement and the right music this method still holds good. However, since arrangers have become accustomed to writing with multitrack techniques in mind, and with the knowledge that extra microphones can be used when required, a new situation has developed. Many big band arrangements can only be performed in a studio; or, if done in concert, spot microphones have to be used. Now, if the amateur is to attempt to record arrangements of this type, it will be of no help to him to use an overall microphone and hope to achieve a balance by playing chess with the musicians. The result will simply be bad tempers all round, a sound which is ill-balanced and playing which at the very least is ragged.

Obviously the amateur cannot emulate a professional studio and use 30 or 40 microphones to give as much individual coverage as required. However, given between six and twelve mixer channels and microphones he should be able to produce a reasonable recording. If microphones are used in close proximity it is worthwhile checking that they are in phase (this is explained in Chapter 7). In general it will be found that the relative phase of the microphones used for multi-mic balancing has little or no subjective effect on the sound quality.

It will usually be found advantageous to split up the orchestra into sections, rather than to have them in the formal visual arrangement used when performing to an audience. Whatever grouping is arrived at, it is important to keep the rhythm section together and in good visual communication—both with each other and with any solo artists. As many microphones as can be spared should be used to cover the rhythm section and some possible layouts are shown. The drum kit should have at least two

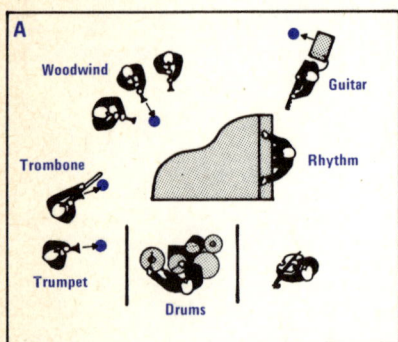

When employing a multi-microphone technique, the band should be split into convenient groups, each group being separately balanced.

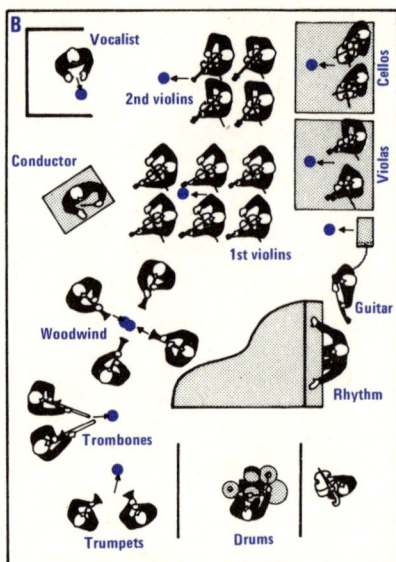

microphones, one overhead in the region of the high hat and the other close to the bass drum. Unless the effect is particularly desired, a ribbon microphone should not be used in close proximity to an instrument such as a bass drum with a high amplitude low frequency output, because of the bass doubling effect. On occasions the technique may produce exactly the sound required, but generally it will have an unpleasant muddy quality.

The double bass can be covered by a microphone close to the strings in the area of the bridge, but many balancers prefer to use a good quality lanyard type of microphone wrapped in foam rubber and located in the fret of the bridge. In this type of balance, a grand piano should be covered with a microphone near the

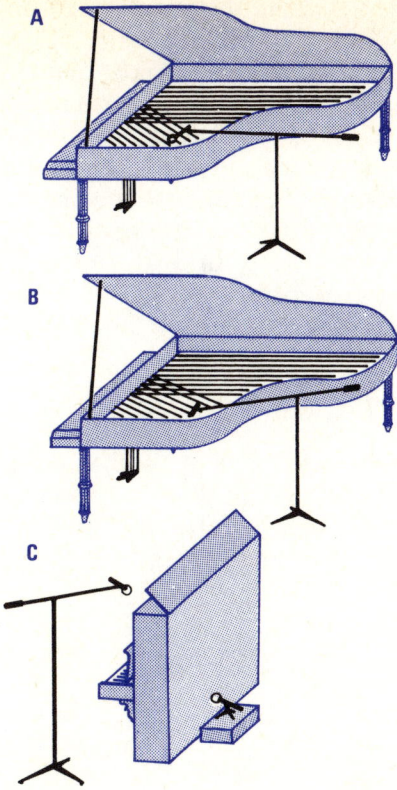

A

B

C

Microphone positions for rhythm piano. If a grand has holes in the iron frame, a microphone placed over hole 2 frequently gives a good balance.

treble strings and the lid should be either open or completely removed. An upright piano can be miked from behind, again with the mic biased towards the high strings, or from above with the top cover open and the microphone poked just inside. Having used as many mics as can reasonably be spared for the rhythm section, the other sections, brass, woodwind, percussion, strings and soloists, should be individually covered. Ideally the sections should be broken down into sub-groups: first and second violins, cellos, trumpets, trombones, saxes, clarinets, flutes and so on, but this is probably out of the question. With only a limited amount of equipment available some compromise is inevitable, and you will have to accept the best balance that can be achieved in the circumstances.

A major problem with this type of recording will be obtaining musical separation between the different instruments. Separation means not the physical space between sections of the orchestra, but the clarity with which each instrument or group of instruments is reproduced. This clarity is diminished if, for instance, the microphone which is covering the flutes also has sound spilling on to it from the brass section or from the drums. The drums can be particularly troublesome in this respect and some form of acoustic screening, as described in Chapter 5, may ease the problem. Each microphone must be placed close to the instrument or group it is covering, so that the associated mic channel on the mixer can be operated at low gain. This has the effect of making the mic less sensitive to the sound spilling over from other instruments. From the foregoing it will be obvious that the best general purpose microphones for music recording are those with a good cardioid characteristic.

Pop Groups

The recording of pop groups is an extension of the big band technique already discussed. Here there will be fewer performers than in a band, but to achieve a good balance it is necessary to give each instrumentalist and vocalist his own microphone. If a

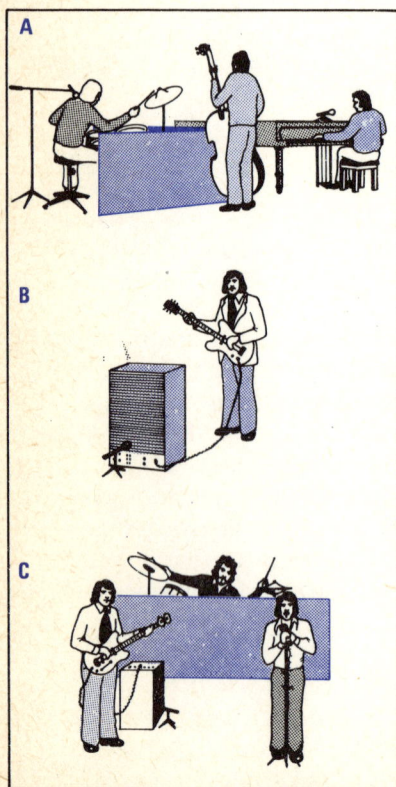

Basic layouts for rhythm and pop groups. In A a low screen is used to separate the bass and drums. In B the electric guitar is covered with a microphone in front of the guitar loudspeaker. In C the drum kit is screened from the guitars and vocalist.

performer both plays and sings he should, where possible, have two mics so that each one can be placed for optimum effect. An exception to this could be the case of a solo performer who sings and accompanies himself on an acoustic guitar: there will then be a natural balance between voice and guitar and a single microphone should be satisfactory.

In general the principles which apply to big band recording also apply to pop work. Maximum separation must be obtained but at the same time the rhythm section must be kept together and in visual contact with the other players. There are so many varied styles of pop and rock music that it is not possible to lay down any firm guidelines about microphone placing. Every session must be approached from scratch and the set-up modified as necessary. Only experience will show what works best in your situation, having regard to the acoustic conditions, the standard of musicianship and the facilities at your disposal. There are several basic layouts, any of which could provide a good starting point from which to begin experimenting. Obviously a pop vocalist will require a robust microphone (definitely not a ribbon) with an effective windshield. Electronic guitar amplifiers should not be fed directly to the mixing desk; instead a microphone should be placed in front of and close to the guitar loudspeaker. This technique can also be used with the electronic organ, but it is only recommended for pop recording where the ensuing coloration is part of the overall sound picture.

Safety

There have been many instances of a pop musician sustaining severe electric shock due to a fault occurring on his electronic instrument. The cause could be a frayed cable, incorrect plug connection or component failure, but the effect is the same—a live chassis. If the performer should then simultaneously touch the instrument and an earth point, such as a microphone stand, his body will provide a path to earth for the mains supply, with possibly fatal consequences. To guard against this possibility, every electronic instrument should be powered via a mains isolating transformer. For maximum safety only one instrument should be powered from each transformer.

Because of the very high sound levels produced in pop music it is important to ensure that the first stage of the mixer, or the tape recorder preamplifier, is not overloaded as this will cause severe 111 distortion. If the level coming out of the microphone is so high that there is very little control on the mixer fader, the signal will have to be attenuated before it reaches the mixer. This is done by inserting a resistor of the appropriate value in the microphone lead—possibly in the plug body. This is a problem which is probably best referred to a reputable hi-fi dealer, as the type of resistive network required will vary according to the equipment used.

Microphone Balance

Having arrived at a satisfactory microphone arrangement, the next thing is to balance the outputs of the various microphones to give a good overall sound texture. As we have seen the ideal situation is for the balance engineer to be in an acoustically isolated room away from the performers so that he can monitor at a realistic level on loudspeakers. In addition to producing an acceptable balance he must also control the dynamic range (or relative loudness) so that the quietest and loudest passages will neither be masked by tape hiss, or ambient noise of the listening room, nor cause distortion through amplifier overload or tape saturation.

With a balance involving more than one microphone, the control of dynamic range is not simply a matter of adjusting the level coming out of the mixer. This is because as the output level is changed, the subjective effect is that the balance has altered. Therefore if a melody line, for instance, is moving from section to section of an orchestra, it will be necessary to follow it with the appropriate microphone faders. With the orchestra in full cry the overall level may have to be pulled down to prevent overload, but this will tend to cause the melody line to be swamped and the fine balance will have been lost. By pulling up the melody slightly the balance will probably be restored. Again, this is not a technique that can easily be described; it is another case of developing a feel for the job.

Listening Level

To achieve a good balance a fairly high listening level should be used and this will also make it easier to detect technical and musical flaws which might otherwise have gone unnoticed until it was too late to rectify them. One of the reasons for monitoring at high level is that the ear's sensitivity to low and to high frequencies falls with reducing level. A correct balance will only be arrived at if the monitoring level approaches that of the live performance. It is not suggested that one should carry this idea to extremes, otherwise partial deafness might ensue, necessitating even higher monitoring levels. There is a grain of truth in the idea that balance engineers are deaf; not that they would admit it—they are simply less sensitive to low sound levels than ordinary mortals!

If it is not possible to monitor on loudspeakers it is worth investing in a really good pair of headphones, probably of the electrostatic type, but this is very much a matter of personal preference. What matters is that they should not be too heavy and that they should be comfortable to wear for long periods. As it is rather easier to damage the hearing when using headphones, care should be taken to ensure that the listening levels are not excessive nor the sessions too lengthy. In time a balancer will find his own preferred level and with experience he will find that he can judge peak levels pretty accurately by ear and rely on the meters more for confirmation.

We have referred to a good balance on many occasions, but how is it arrived at and how do you know when you have got it? The first part of the question is easier to answer. Where there is a main mic and a number of supplementary ones, the first thing is to arrive at a satisfactory coverage from the main one, and then to position and bring in the spot mics one at a time, moving them as necessary until a good, full orchestral sound is achieved. The strings will have 'bite', the brass will be well defined with presence but not harshness; the percussion will have clean transients and there will be a characteristic sharpness or attack to the timpani. It is impossible to describe but you will know when it 'comes together'. When you have it right, note the control settings on a piece of paper lest some idiot decides to experiment whilst you are out of the room.

With pop and multi-mic balances, each instrument or group of instruments must first be listened to individually and the mics set as required. The balance is then built up section by section starting with the rhythm group. There should be as little spill-over of sound as possible from one instrumental group to another. It may be necessary to adjust the physical layout of the orchestra to achieve this but the musicians must always be at ease when playing.

Echo

A major problem for the amateur is to create the right type of echo effect. In a studio this echo—or artificial reverberation as it is more properly known—is usually derived from an expensive reverberation plate or from a spring device. The amateur is limited either to the use of one of the rudimentary spring systems which are commercially available or to the use of a tape delay system. Either device can be useful for pop vocalists or for filling out the brass sound of a band, but both are very limited in application as the same percentage of echo has to be added to everything indiscriminately. Only an expensive and complex mixer has separate echo mixture switches on each channel so that the percentage of reverberation added to each channel can be individually controlled.

For classical and much light orchestral work it is better to derive the reverberation by using one or two cardioid microphones towards the back of the hall, facing the orchestra. The output of these microphones is then mixed into the main balance until the optimum sound texture is achieved. In a fairly dead hall this technique can be very effective but take care not to be over-enthusiastic about it and overdo the effect. First establish the initial balance without reverberation and only worry about it when everything else is right. In many cases, of course, the opposite problem will apply and the acoustic of the hall will be too live. Drapes and screens may help to a limited extent but there is no real answer to an unsatisfactory hall. The chances are that the microphones will have to be placed closer than is desirable for orchestral work in order to improve the ratio of direct to indirect sound.

Of all the topics discussed in this book, the art of music recording is the most difficult to reduce to any kind of formula. In the realm of speech recording there are certain techniques, as we have seen, which by common consent are applicable to certain recording situations. In music there is far more room for manoeuvre—and thus for error. There is also more controversy about sound balance and the placing of microphones.

9. Editing

There is something special about tape editing. Its fascination is such that some enthusiasts specialise in creating programmes by using this particular craft almost to the exclusion of live voices or musicians. Part of the attraction of tape editing is that it is a one-man operation (or two at the most) and thus there is no conflict of interest. The editor can apply his own skill in his own way. He can work without compromise and he can take as much time as he wishes to obtain a specific result. A professional editor may work more quickly and confidently but he is always fighting the clock. Editing is therefore the only aspect of creative recording where the amateur has a chance of meeting the professional on equal terms. The professional will invariably turn out a competent piece of work; the amateur will frequently fail but just once in a while he may approach perfection.

Editing is one of the most rewarding and creative of recording activities. There is a feeling of satisfaction when a project is successfully completed, rarely experienced during the recording session. This is largely because the work is unfinished until the editing is done. A recording session is a sort of foreshortened pregnancy, whilst the edited tape is the baby! Editing is, in fact, a combination of two very different skills, both of which are of equal importance. The first is the ability to locate an editing point and to cut and splice sections of tape with precision. The second is the ability to listen objectively to a series of recordings and to know instinctively which sections will cut together to give the desired result. Sometimes a person will have the one ability but not the other, which is why editing can be a two-man operation.

The Editing Machine

Over the years professional tape editors have developed a specialised approach to their work and machines have been designed with their needs in mind. A professional tape machine, for instance, will have an uncluttered deck with very few control knobs, switches or levers in close proximity to the head block. The tape path will be a simple arc so that the tape can be threaded with a single movement of the hand. Very few domestic or even semi-professional machines offer ideal conditions for editing, and it is essential not to underestimate the importance of operational convenience when looking for a new machine. Editing on an unsuitable deck can be a form of abbreviated purgatory and many enthusiasts have been deterred because of early experiences with cheap domestic decks—and 5 in (13 cm) spools!

For editing purposes the deck should always be fitted with the largest spools it will accept, but in the pause and stop modes it will probably be difficult to move the spools by hand because of the braking action. The answer in that case is to find a combination of the tape transport switches which will release the brakes without engaging fast wind or play; or alternatively the deck can be suitably modified. One possibility is to select play and then partially apply the pause control until the tape just stops. If the control is wedged in this position, the brakes should be free, allowing the tape to be moved easily by hand whilst the output is monitored either on a loudspeaker or headphones. A few machines are fitted with a switch which mutes the replay amplifier unless the play mode is selected. If you have to edit on a machine of this type it will be necessary to override the muting switch.

To improve tape handling for editing the following techniques can be used: A, select PLAY to release brakes and PAUSE to disengage tape drive. B, thread tape *behind* capstan and select PLAY. C, modify deck and fit reel motor inhibit switch (see text).

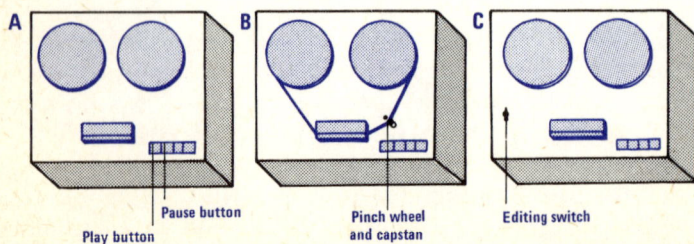

Play button
Pause button
Pinch wheel and capstan
Editing switch

Another technique to simplify tape handling is to thread the tape on the wrong side of the capstan, and to select play. The brakes will release but because the tape is not being driven it will remain stationary and under slight tension from the take-up motor. This technique will not work with all machines, but an alternative, which can be tried with a number of three-motor decks, is to fit an *edit* switch. This entails a certain amount of rewiring, will almost certainly invalidate the guarantee and may need the assistance of a knowledgeable friend. The idea is to insert a switch in the mains feed to the spool motors. This switch is normally closed—when the operation of the machine is unchanged—but when opened, the mains feed is broken. If fast wind is selected with the edit switch open, the brakes will release but the spool motors will not be energised, which is ideal for editing.

Of course it is possible, with a little ingenuity, to edit tape on virtually any machine, but if you are to enjoy serious creative work, the physical matter of cutting and splicing must be made easy. It is worth browsing through the classified advertisements in the trade journals and trying to locate an old studio machine which is being sold off. It may not be much good as a recording or playback machine, but provided a reasonable output can be obtained for monitoring it should be ideal for editing.

Marking the Tape

Assuming that a domestic or semi-professional deck is being used, and that some method has been arrived at of moving the tape by hand without waging war with the braking system, the next thing is to ensure that the tape can be marked and cut with a minimum of difficulty. Ideally it should be possible to mark the tape with the edit point against the replay head, which is one reason pressure pads should be avoided. If pressure pads are fitted it may be possible, temporarily, to remove the tension spring from the pressure arm and swing it out of the way. Or, with a minor modification, it may be possible to make the pressure arm quickly detachable and to remove it during editing sessions. Time spent devising some means of marking the tape at the replay head will be amply repaid by the saving of frustration on those evenings when everything seems to go wrong.

If, despite your ingenuity, the replay head remains inaccessible, the answer is to use an *offset* mark. The idea is to measure accurately the distance between the replay head gap and the chosen marking point (say the right-hand tape guide). This 117 measurement—which we will call *A*—is then transferred to the editing block by scribing a line at distance *A* to the right of the razor channel. When an edit point is found, the tape is marked at the right-hand tape guide. This mark is then placed over the scribed offset mark on the editing block and the tape is cut in the usual manner.

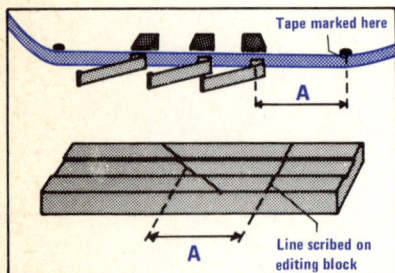

If the replay head is inaccessible an 'offset' mark will have to be used for tape editing. Measure the distance 'A' from replay head to marking point and transfer this measurement to editing block, as shown.

The most useful marking device is the Chinagraph or wax pencil, and for years yellow was all that was needed. However, there are now so many different shades of oxide and of base material in use that other colours are also required. Yellow and blue are the most useful colours and show up distinctly on many tapes, but occasionally red, or possibly green, may be required. To mark an edit point, the tape is first played through at normal speed so that the cutting point can be confirmed. The tape is then re-wound and the spools rocked to and fro by hand so that the tape see-saws across the heads. When the cutting point is identified, by ear, the

Use a consistent marking method, either slightly above or slightly below the centre of the tape.

see-saw action is slowed down until the chosen point rests on the replay head. The tape is then marked by pressing the point of a wax crayon against it, either opposite the replay head or against an offset mark. The tape should always be marked in the same manner, either slightly above or slightly below centre. If sequences are subsequently mixed up on several spools, it is immediately apparent if a particular sequence is spooled *tail in* or *tail out*.

118

The Cutting Point

At first it is hard to identify sounds when the tape is moved slowly and the inexperienced editor should play the marked tape through at normal speed before cutting it, to confirm that the mark is correct. With speech the gaps between words produce no output when the tape is rocked, or if they do it is due to hum or tape noise and is at very low level. Having found the required gap, the tape is eased on until the start of the next word is found. It is then moved back slightly so that the cut is made just before the word begins. If this is done as a matter of course, the natural rhythm of the speech will be preserved; whereas if cuts are made

Editing points where there is a pause

When editing out a 'fluff', use the natural pause left by the speaker.

random fashion during pauses, the edited tape will give the speech an unreal jerky delivery. With practice it will be found possible not only to cut out unwanted words but also to remove syllables from mispronounced words. With music, the cutting point is dictated by the tempo and structure of the music, and it is important that in addition to sounding correct, the edit point makes sense in the context of the music. If the tape should be marked inaccurately, say halfway through a bar instead of at the beginning of it, this will not be apparent provided the mistake is repeated at the subsequent cut—the edit will simply have been moved forward half a bar.

Remember that the perfect edit is inaudible. Every documentary, gramophone record, and almost every recorded radio talk is edited, but the listener is rarely aware of the fact. It does not matter how much is cut out provided that the natural flow is maintained, that the character and sense are preserved and that one faithfully represents what the speaker intended to say.

Editing Techniques

It is usually good policy to be bold when editing. The tape should be marked quickly and cut with confidence—the aim should be to get the edit right first time. Occasionally things will go wrong, but the tape can always be patched back together for another attempt. A typical problem is the speaker who runs words together: 'Yes-er, Iyum, think-er believe this is the right 119 approach.' To edit this down to: 'Yes, I believe this is the right approach,' can be a tricky operation, particularly separating the 'Yes' and the 'I', and it may be necessary to 'nibble' at the tape on either side of the join, taking off a fraction at a time and re-splicing the tape until it sounds right. If a tape is likely to prove difficult, or you are not too sure of your own ability, it is advisable to copy the original and to edit the copy.

Many amateurs go wrong after they have marked the tape, as a result of which they make splicing a laborious operation. They lift the tape clear of the heads and out of the head block before putting it in the splicing block; the tape must then be re-laced after each edit. It is much better to move the marked tape through to the right of the head block and then to pull a loop of tape

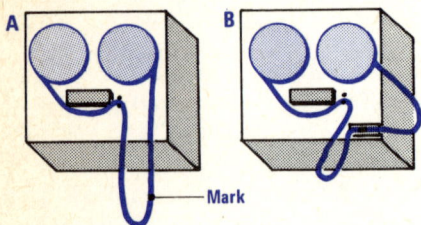

Editing procedure: A, mark the tape and pull out a loop of tape, to the right of the head block. B, place mark on the editing block. Cut and pull out unwanted tape. Make splice and tape is ready threaded.

forward for editing. When the unwanted material has been pulled out and the tape spliced, the slack is simply taken up and you are immediately ready to start looking for the next edit point. From this it should be obvious that the most logical and operationally most convenient place for the editing block is forward and to the right of the tape heads. This is where it will be found on virtually all professional machines, but for some reason best known to themselves, manufacturers of domestic, and many semi-professional, recorders have other ideas. Frequently there is no provision of any kind for the fitting of a block; or if one can be fitted it is often in an unsatisfactory position—such as on top of the head block—which necessitates unthreading the tape every time an edit is made. It is well worth making a simple jig so that an editing block can be fixed, if only temporarily, to the front right-hand side of the tape deck.

Typical editing block as used in recording and broadcasting studios. Slightly under-cut channel grips tape ready for cutting.

Splicing Block

The ideal editing (or splicing) block is one which enables the operator to cut and join the tape with a minimum of effort. In broadcasting and recording studios a block is used in which the tape is gripped in the long channel which is slightly undercut, and there are razor guides at 45° and 90° to the tape. Editing can quickly be accomplished if the tape is eased into the channel with the forefinger of each hand and then sliced with a single-edged razor blade. After a little practice the action of putting the tape into the block and cutting it becomes refined into a single continuous action. For speed and simplicity this type of block is peerless. However, as the tape itself has to undergo quite an amount of manhandling when editing, it is prudent to use the thicker standard play tape for creative work, which is less liable to curl or stretch than the thinner ones.

It is generally easier to cut the tape if it is held firmly with a finger placed either side of the razor guide whilst the blade is drawn along it. For most purposes the 45° angle should be used as this is less likely to produce an audible click when the tape is replayed. Some old time editors use brass scissors for cutting the tape and, remarkably, always manage to cut it at the same angle.

Making the Joint

The most suitable splicing tape is the narrow ¼ in (6.25 mm) type which lies along the tape. The ends to be joined are simply butted together and a length of splicing tape is pressed on top of them. On no account should ordinary adhesive tape be used for this purpose as the adhesive will ooze over a period of time.

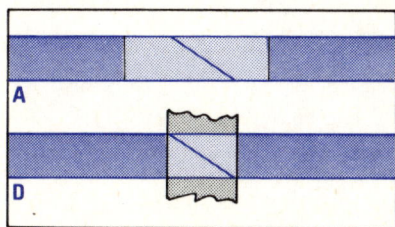

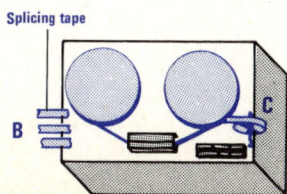

Splicing. A, butt ends of tape together and cover with longitudinal patch of splicing tape (¼ in (6.25 mm) wide). B, some editors pre-cut a series of lengths of splicing tape and fix them to the machine, ready for use. C, alternatively, the free end of the splicing tape roll can be attached to a chrome handle. The free end is cut off when a splice is made and the roll unwound slightly. D, transverse patches of splicing tape which have to be trimmed to size are not recommended.

121

This will cause adjacent layers of tape to stick together and will also cause a sticky deposit to be left on the tape heads. Many editors cut a number of 1 in (25 mm) lengths of splicing tape at the beginning of an editing session and attach them to the edge of the deck by one corner: they are then ready for instant use when a splice is to be made. However, if too many strips are cut in advance the adhesive may start drying out and the joints could pull apart later. An alternative method of making quick joints is to mount a chromed handle on the right-hand side of the deck and to stick the free end of the roll of splicing tape to it, leaving a couple of inches protruding. Each time a joint is made a piece of the free splicing tape is cut off and the roll is unwound a little, ready for the next edit. The use of ½ in (13 mm) wide splicing tape, which is placed across the join and then trimmed to size, makes the operation time consuming and tedious and is not recommended for serious work.

The only way to master the physical side of editing is to do a great deal of it, and the easiest way to begin is by chopping up pieces of tape and joining them together again. Given a degree of manual dexterity the mechanical operation can quickly be learned. A good exercise is to go through your tape collection and to edit a length of leader tape on to the beginning and end of each reel. The start leader should be cut as close as possible to the beginning of the recording, whilst the end leader should follow several seconds after the end of the recording to allow for the atmosphere to be faded out. There are many pitfalls in editing, many of which only become apparent when you have ruined what could have been a very good production. Usually a particular mistake is only made once, but that can be quite enough—especially if it is a friend's tape you have just ruined. If your editing skills are rudimentary, remember the earlier advice and copy any valuable material.

There are a number of reasons for editing a tape, the most obvious of which is to remove something which is incorrect and to substitute a re-take. This applies equally to speech or music recording and the basic sequence has already been described. But creative recording is very much more than simply cutting out mistakes. It was said earlier that it is a combination of two skills, manual dexterity and mental agility. This second skill is a nebulous one: it calls for a mind which can imagine how a cut will sound before it is made. It also calls for a clear mind which can envisage the form of the end product during the embryo stage when takes are scattered on a number of separate spools.

Speech

Broadly, there are three categories of editing: speech, music and sound effects, and we will consider them in that order. Speech may be scripted or unscripted, but the basic techniques are common to both. We have already suggested that it is important to maintain the natural delivery of a speaker so that, although we take out many of the 'ums' and 'ahs', we do not turn him into an automaton. Nor, to be natural, should we remove all the hesitations: we should take out enough to improve the fluency and make the tape easier on the ear.

If several sentences are being taken out, it is important to decide if the pause at the edit point represents the end of a sentence or a paragraph: this should be clear from the context or the script. In order to ensure that the pause is a natural one, play the tape at normal speed to establish the rhythm of the speech, then stop the tape and mark it when the pause feels right. If a long pause is needed, use some of the studio atmosphere recorded at the end of the tape—see Chapter 6. The same chapter also recommends a technique which should be followed when recording re-takes for subsequent editing.

One of the pitfalls in speech editing is the *double breath*. Most speakers make an audible intake of breath at the beginning of a sentence and it is quite natural to leave such breaths in the edited tape. However, when editing two sentences together—if a consistent marking technique is not used—it is very easy to end up with a pause which has a double breath, and it sounds very peculiar. This type of editing is more difficult to describe than it is to perform and most amateur recordists can quickly become proficient at it.

Assembly work is rather more difficult and the sound documentary, as with the film, is made on the editing block. The linking narration and the various interviews are the bare bones. The creative work lies in building the bones into a frame and giving the frame life. Using the same material, one editor will produce a tape which bores his audience silly and another will produce a fascinating investigation. The art lies in imaginative and intelligent selection and in clever juxtaposition. Harden your pocket against the cost of tape and be ruthless with your editing. It's what you throw away that makes the difference between a good and a poor production. Try to maintain interest, pace and vocal contrast, and do not let any voice continue for longer than it can hold the listener's attention. 'Pace' does not mean that the production should proceed at breakneck speed, but rather that a particular theme—whether drama or documentary—has a natural rhythm dictated by the content and treatment. This is not something which can be defined but it is the very essence of this craft: pace is a matter of instinct and interpretation and is worth seeking.

When assembling the final or 'production' tape, it is helpful if a number of empty spools are available, one of which will be used for building up the production tape in sequence. If the

When assembling complex sequences from several reels of tape a numbered rack above the machine is useful for identifying the various spools.

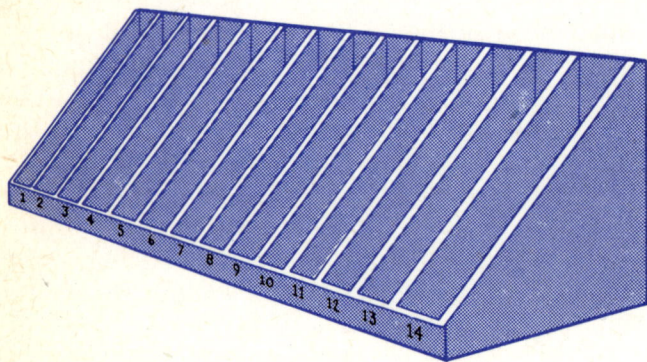

production tape is to be assembled from a number of separate tapes, it is a good idea to number the tapes and to stand them vertically in a rack above the recorder. The numbering of the tapes should correspond with their identification in the script. The required spools can then be selected and edited in turn and the scrap material wound off on to one of the empty spools.

If sequences are put together in this way, the production tape can either be edited to its final form as you go along, or a rough cut can be done, just to get the order correct, and the precise editing can be done later. Much depends on the complexity of the particular production. If two tape machines are available it often saves a great deal of time when assembling sequences, if the rough cut is done by *dub-editing*. In this system the required sections are copied in sequence on to a blank tape and the artistic work is done

124   afterwards.

A coloured leader or trailer tape should be used to identify the beginning and end of each recording and it helps to avoid confusion if a coding system is adopted, such as yellow for the beginning and red for the end. For dramatic work, when assembling insert tapes, if the leader tape is used with the matt side away from the heads it is possible to write on it with a soft pencil to identify sequences. But beware! some types of splicing tape do not stick too well to matt backings and it is rather embarrassing if a joint falls apart just before a tape is cued.

With recordings of unscripted talks or interviews it is necessary to work from memory and by instinct—or to have a transcript made of the tape. If you have a friend who is a competent shorthand typist, then you have a valuable asset, as it is far easier to work out what to cut if a transcript is available. The physical editing operation is also much simplified if the script is clearly marked, showing which sequences are to be cut together. Be sure to note a speaker's intonation at a proposed edit point because, although the edited version may read naturally, it may sound odd if a sentence begins or ends on a wrong inflexion.

Music

Music editing is done for three basic reasons: to shorten or extend a piece of music, to correct an error, or for the assembly and creation of electronic music. The first of these is of use mainly in drama, although the same technique can be used in film documentary to make a piece of music last for the duration of a particular visual sequence. The idea is to become familiar with the music by repeated playing and to note the overall form of the arrangement. Many popular tunes, for instance, are based on eight- or sixteen-bar sequences and there is frequently repetition of a theme or a rhythmic pattern. Having analysed the music make a mental note of how the bar sequences are linked and if necessary draw the structure on a sheet of paper and mark possible cutting points.

Shortening the music is relatively easy: all you have to do is to find a phrase which can be removed without noticeably disturbing the musical pattern. For example, if a tune has the following structure: 4 bars introduction, 24 bars melody (including an 8-bar bridge passage) and 4 bars closing, it may be possible to cut from bar 21 to bar 28, the actual cutting points being just before the first beat of bars 21 and 29. This type of editing is obviously only effective on the more lightweight and predictable types of tune. It is less likely to be successful or even desirable to treat Beethoven in this cavalier fashion!

To lengthen the same piece of music it is necessary first of all to copy the entire tune on to another tape, and then to copy several times over the section from bars 21 to 28. All the subsequent editing is done on the copy tape so the levels at the cutting points should match. The complete tune is cut just before the first beat of bar 21 and a new section is inserted, which is in fact one of the copied extracts of bars 21 to 28. At the end of the extract, bar 29 of the original tape is joined on and this leads into the end sequence.

With this type of editing it is essential to choose the cutting points wisely and to ensure that the physical cuts are accurate. For example, if the bar count or basic rhythm is disturbed, or if the tempo or loudness change abruptly at the join, the edit will be a failure. Provided the correct cutting points are found the music can be extended indefinitely for as long as the listener can stand the monotony. The important thing, of course, is that editing to time in this manner is usually done because the music is an accompaniment to dialogue, action or visual effect. Therefore no one is listening critically to the music; it is merely setting atmosphere and provided the edit points pass muster, the technique will work.

When music has to be edited to correct errors made during the recording session, many of the same considerations apply as those for speech recording. It is essential that the re-take is of sufficient length to allow the players to recapture the feel of the music, and it should also be long enough to give a choice of cutting points. The balance must be identical to the original recording, the microphone placings must be unchanged and all mixer and tape recorder controls should be on the correct gain settings. Provided the re-take is properly recorded, music is no more difficult to edit than speech; except that it does require a sufficiently good ear to find a given point in the music fairly readily. The ability to read a score is useful but by no means essential: if your ear recognises musical patterns and phrases and can remember them, that is sufficient.

Tape Loops

One very useful effect—mentioned briefly in Chapter 7—is the
tape loop. To make a loop, several seconds of the required effect

should be copied. The tape is then cut to a rather longer length than required and left laced through the heads. If one end of the length of tape is held in each hand, the tape can be see-sawed across the heads. The tape is then marked in two points where the sound is identical, and which are far enough apart to give a loop

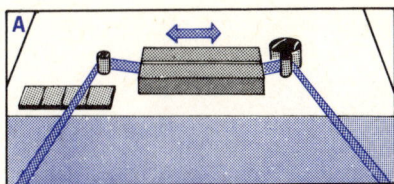

To make a tape loop copy a length of the required repetitive effect. Cut the tape longer than required and hold it by the cut ends. Rock the tape across the heads and make two marks some distance apart, where the sound is identical. Cut as marked and form loop. A large loop will need weighting to maintain tension on the tape. A patch cord serves well for this purpose.

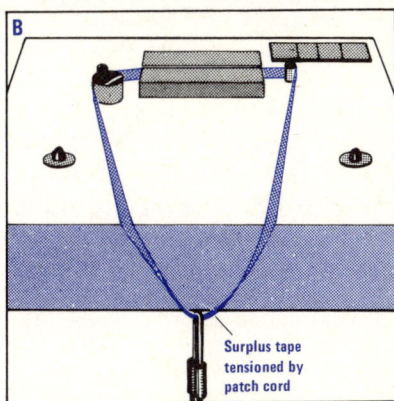

Surplus tape tensioned by patch cord

of suitable length when the ends are joined together. In order to replay the tape satisfactorily the loop should be maintained under tension, and the spools should be removed allowing the hubs to run free.

A refinement of the loop idea can be used if, say, a motor car tick-over, or some other repetitive noise, has to continue for an indefinite time and then abruptly change on a given cue. Again a loop is used for the repetitive sound but another tape machine is set up with just a second of the repetitive sound on the tape, followed by the noise of the car driving off, or whatever development is appropriate. What happens is that the tape loop runs throughout the scene for as long as required and on cue the second machine is started, with its fader open to a predetermined level. As the second machine is started with one hand, the tape loop is rapidly faded out with the other.

The sound of a machine running down or starting up can be difficult to obtain and one way of simulating the effect is to obtain 127 a commercial record of the running machine and to copy it to tape. After this, experiment with the gram unit and find out what sound is produced if the effects record is played whilst the turntable motor is switched off and on at the mains. If you edit the resultant effect on to the previously recorded continuous run, it could well give a close approximation to the required sound.

Sound Montage

In Chapter 7 we mentioned the assembly of sound montages. All these require are two or three tape recorders and a gram unit—and sufficient imagination to combine a few simple effects to produce an altogether different impression. A basic atmosphere is copied from the gram unit to track one of the first tape machine (M/C1). The tape is rewound and another effects track is recorded on track two of M/C1. Both tracks of the tape on M/C1 are now mixed and copied to track one of M/C2, whilst further effects are added from the gram unit. A new effect is now added to track two of M/C2 and the composite tape is rewound and copied to track one of M/C1 with further effects added from the gram unit. M/C1 is now rewound and another new effect is recorded on track two. This process can be repeated until the tape noise becomes excessive and some quite remarkable sound effects can be produced.

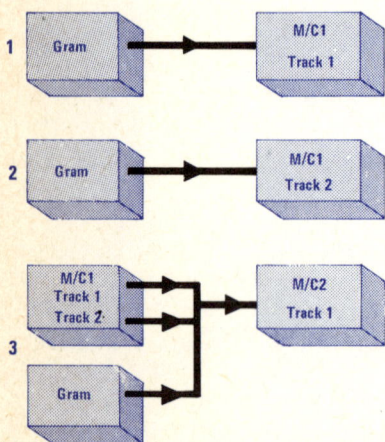

Making a sound montage. A repeated copying technique is used. A gram effect is recorded on machine 1 (M/C 1), track 1. Tape rewound, second effect recorded on track 2. M/C 1 rewound and replayed, tracks 1 and 2 are mixed and further grams added and recorded on M/C 2, track 1, and so on until the montage is complete.

It is important to remember that both tracks of a stereo recorder can be used independently. For instance if you want a ship at sea to be overtaken by a storm, the normal sea effects can be recorded on track one and the storm effects on track two. At the beginning of the scene the machine is played with track one only faded up.

As the storm develops track two is gradually faded in until the storm sound overrides that of track one.

If both tracks are used it is necessary to ensure that only one of these requires editing. The track to be edited is then recorded first and when the editing is completed, the second track is recorded. If the joints are well made and a speed of 7½in/s (19cm/s) is used, they should not noticeably affect the quality of the effects recorded on the other track. Use of spliced tape for recording serious music is not recommended.

This chapter, like the rest of the book, has merely introduced the reader to a particular topic. There has been no attempt to discuss it exhaustively, because that would have required a different type of book. There is no great mystery about recording or the allied arts and the secret of success lies in mastering a few basic techniques. The magic is in the achievement of an end product and in the minds of those whose creative endeavours bring it to life. Recording is not a passive activity and our object throughout has been to encourage the reader to experiment. The sound medium offers unrivalled freedom to the imagination—use it!

Appendix

For English Readers

Recommended Books

The Technique of the Sound Studio, Alec Nisbett, Focal Press
The Use of Microphones, Alec Nisbett, Focal Press
Tape Recorders, H. W. Hellyer, Fountain Press
The Audio Handbook, Gordon J. King, Newnes-Butterworths
Master Stereo Cassette Recording, I. R. Sinclair, Newnes-Butterworths
Master Hi-Fi Installation, Gordon J. King, Newnes-Butterworths
Pickups and Loudspeakers, John Earl, Fountain Press
Tuners and Amplifiers, John Earl, Fountain Press
Audio Technician's Bench Manual, John Earl, Fountain Press
Hi-Fi Year Book, IPC Electrical-Electronic Year Books Ltd, published each autumn

Useful Periodicals

Practical Hi-Fi and Audio (IPC) Monthly
Practical Electronics (IPC) Monthly
Wireless World (IPC) Monthly
Studio Sound (Link House) Monthly
Hi-Fi News (Link House) Monthly

Test Tapes

Agfa-Gevaert Ltd., Great West Road, Brentford, Middlesex
BASF (UK) Ltd., Audio/Video Tapes Division, P.O. Box 473, Knightsbridge House, 197, Knightsbridge, London, SW7 1SA

EMI Sound and Vision Equipment Ltd., 252, Blyth Road, Hayes, UB3 1HW

Tutchings Electronics Ltd., 14, Rook Hill Road, Friars Cliff, Christchurch

Test Records

Decca Record Co. Ltd., 9, Albert Embankment, London, SE1 7SW. SKL 4861, *How To Give Yourself a Stereo Checkout*

EMI Records Ltd, EMI House, 20, Manchester Square, London, W1. TCS 101, TCS 102, TCS 104, TCS 105, *Frequency Response Tests*

Hi-Fi Sound, Test Record HFS 75, distributed through: Howland-West Ltd., 3–5 Eden Grove, London, N7 8EQ

Microphones and Accessories

Adastra Electronics Ltd., Unit N22, Cricklewood Trading Estate, Claremont Road, London, NW2 1TU

AKG Equipment Ltd., Eardley House, 182–184 Campden Hill Road, Kensington, London, W8 7AS

Beyer Dynamic (GB) Ltd., 1 Clair Road, Haywards Heath, Sussex

Eagle International, Heather Park Drive, Wembley, HA0 1SU

Electro-Voice, Gulton Europe Ltd., Special Products Division, The Hyde, Brighton, BN2 4JU

Gardners Transformers Ltd., Christchurch, Dorset, BH23 3PN

Grampian Reproducers Ltd., 19, Hanworth Trading Estate. Hampton Road West, Feltham, TW13 6EJ

Reslosound Ltd., Spring Gardens, London Road, Romford, Essex, RM7 9LJ

Sennheiser, Hayden Laboratories Ltd., Hayden House, 17, Chesham Road, Amersham, Bucks., HP6 5AG

Shure Electronics Ltd., Eccleston Road, Maidstone, Kent, ME15 6AU

STC: distributed by Hampstead High Fidelity, 91, Heath Road, Hampstead, London, NW3

Tape Accessories

Audio Packs (connectors and adaptors), Tape Recorder Spares Ltd., 206–210, Ilderton Road, London, SE15 1NS

Bib Hi-Fi Accessories Ltd., P.O. Box 78, Hemel Hempstead, Herts.

BASF (splicing tape, editing kits, leader tape), address as given on page 131

Metrosound Audio Products Ltd., Cartersfield Road, Waltham
   Abbey, Essex, EN9 1JF
QAS (adaptors and leads), Wollaton Road, Beeston, Nottingham,
   NG9 2PB

Tape Amplifiers and Mixer Units

Adastra Electronics Ltd., address as given on page 132
Audio Developments, Hall Lane, Walsall Wood, Staffs.,
   WS9 9AU
Brenell Engineering Co Ltd., 231–235 Liverpool Road, London,
   N1 1LY
Eagle International, address as given on page 132
H/H Electronic, Industrial Site, Cambridge Road, Milton,
   Cambridge, CB4 4AZ
Millbank Electronics Ltd., Bellbrook Estate, Uckfield, Sussex,
   TN22 1PS
Uher (UK) Ltd., 15 Broomhills Estate, Braintree, Essex,
   CM7 7RQ
Vortexion, 257–263, The Broadway, Wimbledon, London,
   SW19 1SF

Sound Effects Records

Manufactured by: EMI, BBC, Pye, Argo and available through
   record retailers.
In particular see EMI and BBC catalogues for atmospheres and
   dramatic effects. Argo catalogue does not list sound effects as
   such but many train recordings, speeches, plays, poetry
   readings and historic events are available and can be used to
   good purpose.

Organisations

Federation of British Tape Recording Clubs (FBTRC). PRO:
   John Bradley, 33, Fairlawnes, Maldon Road, Wallington,
   Surrey. Quarterly magazine: *News and Views*
Audio Engineering Society. Secretary, 32, Knoll Rise, Orpington,
   Kent, BR6 0EL
British Kinematograph, Sound and Television Society, Secretary,
   110/112, Victoria House, Vernon Place, London, WC1B 4DJ

Amateur Competition

The British Amateur Tape Recording Contest (held annually).
   Contest Secretary, 33, Fairlawnes, Maldon Road,
   Wallington, Surrey

For American Readers

Recommended Books

Hi-Fi Loudspeakers and Enclosures, A. Cohen, Hayden
Master Hi-Fi Installation, Gordon J. King, Hayden
Master Stereo Cassette Recording, I. R. Sinclair, Hayden
Quad Sound, M. Tepper, Hayden

Useful Periodicals

Audio Magazine, Monthly
Hi-Fidelity Magazine, Monthly
Stereo Review, Monthly

Test Tapes

Ampex Corporation
AEG-Telefunken, Gotham Audio Corporation, 741 Washington
    St., New York, NY 10014
CBS Laboratories, Stamford, Connecticut
BASF Systems, Crosby Drive, Bedford, Mass. 01730

Test Records

CBS Laboratories, Stamford, Connecticut
London Records Inc., New York

Microphones and Accessories

Shure Bros. Inc., 222, Hartrey Avenue, Evanston, Ill. 60204
Electro-voice Inc., 603, Cecil St. Buchanan, Michigan 49107
AKG: distributed by Philips Audio Video Systems Corporation,
    Audio Division, 91, McKee Drive, Mahwah, New Jersey,
    07430
Neumann, Gotham Audio Corporation, 741 Washington St.,
    New York, NY 10014

Amplifier and Mixer Units

Heath Co. Dept., 41-11, Benton Harbor, Michigan 49022
TEAC Corporation, 7733 Telegraph Road, Montebello,
    CA 90640

Organisations

Audio Engineering Society Inc., Room 449, 60 E. 42nd St. New
    York, NY 10017

Index

135